THE WORKS OF HAROLD J. LASKI

Volume 13

I0883817

THE STRATEGY OF FREEDOM

THE STRATEGY OF FREEDOM

An Open Letter to Students especially American

HAROLD J. LASKI

Routledge
Taylor & Francis Group
LONDON AND NEW YORK

First published 1942 by George Allen & Unwin Ltd

2 Park Square, Milton Park, Abingdon, Oxfordshire OX14 4RN
711 Third Avenue, New York, NY 10017

Routledge is an imprint of the Taylor & Francis Group, an informa business

First issued in paperback 2018

Copyright © 1942 Taylor & Francis

All rights reserved. No part of this book may be reprinted or reproduced or utilised in any form or by any electronic, mechanical, or other means, now known or hereafter invented, including photocopying and recording, or in any information storage or retrieval system, without permission in writing from the publishers.

Notice:
Product or corporate names may be trademarks or registered trademarks, and are used only for identification and explanation without intent to infringe.

British Library Cataloguing in Publication Data
A catalogue record for this book is available from the British Library

ISBN: 978-1-138-81912-2 (Set)
ISBN: 978-1-138-82219-1 (hbk) (Volume 13)
ISBN: 978-1-138-82307-5 (pbk) (Volume 13)

Publisher's Note
The publisher has gone to great lengths to ensure the quality of this reprint but points out that some imperfections in the original copies may be apparent.

Disclaimer
The publisher has made every effort to trace copyright holders and would welcome correspondence from those they have been unable to trace.

The Strategy of Freedom

An Open Letter to Students especially American

by

HAROLD J. LASKI

LONDON
George Allen & Unwin Ltd

First published in 1942

All rights reserved

Made and Printed in Great Britain by
Billing and Sons Ltd., Guildford and Esher

FOR FELIX

1916-41

H.

One

All over the world, wherever there are free men and women, the desire for the defeat of Hitlerism and its allies is passionate and profound. Ordinary people who, in the normal course of things, hate war have recognised that if, in this conflict, Great Britain were to be defeated, something like a dark age would settle down upon mankind. What, they are convinced, is in hazard are certain fundamental principles of civilisation —the rule of law against the power of arbitrary discretion, the right to freedom of the mind against the power of outlaws to control the direction of thought, the co-operation of nations by way of free association instead of by coercive subordination. Each time a stand has been taken against the relentless tyranny of the dictators, whether it has been Matteoti in Rome or Dimitroff in Berlin, whether it has been Britain after the fall of France or Greece and Jugoslavia insisting on battle rather than upon surrender, the conscience of the whole free world has been lit by a new gleam of hope. Even in India, where an unresolved conflict between the British Government and the national leaders haunts the scene like a grim shadow, there is none of those leaders who does not admit that the defeat of Britain would end, for a long period to come, the hope of Indian freedom. For they know that a German victory in the West may spell Japanese domination in the East; and the history of China in the last eight years has revealed something of the price men have to pay for Japanese domination.

An Englishman is bound to note with pride the growth in the United States of sympathy with, and aid for, the cause for which our people are fighting. The call for that sympathy and aid has transcended all boundaries of class or creed or party; it has triumphed over historical misunderstandings and surviving scepticisms as deep as any in the modern world. Those who have sought to halt its full expression have been felt to misunderstand the central principles upon which the American way of life has been built. They have been felt to deny the creative rôle it is the duty of an America to play which hopes to retain for herself a civilisation assured of freedom and democracy. Sometimes their opposition has been the outcome of genuine intellectual error. Sometimes, humanly enough, it has been born of a pacifist philosophy to which the maintenance of freedom by the method of war is the supreme mistake in state policy. Sometimes it is the consequence of more sinister motives, directly born of the power of the dictators to purchase support for their evil ends.

I have an association which goes back over twenty-five years with American universities. I have taught in many of them; teachers and students in many have been among the closest of my friends. In the years of my own residence in the United States, if I had to make a criticism of American students, it would have been of regret at their aloofness from the political scene about them. Save at the dramatic moment of a Presidential election, it was rare for more than a small handful of them to realise that universities are not ivory towers, remote from the main stream of social life, but watch-towers which have no meaning save as they closely guard, and carefully register, the significance of a civilisation whose trends they are bound to express.

It was, therefore, to me an exciting thing when, about the time of the Great Depression in the United States, there was an unmistakable stirring on every university campus I have visited. Groups of students, growing ever larger as the years went by, began increasingly to understand how deeply they were involved in the crisis of our civilisation, how impossible it was for them not to demand that academic life should confront its implications with courage. It was a heartening thing to see them growingly determined to penetrate to the roots of this crisis. It was exhilarating to see them not only flock to the class-rooms of those teachers prepared to analyse its meaning without deference to the vested interests which feared the results of such analysis, but, even more, quick to defend those teachers when the vested interests sought their penalisation. Above all, between 1933 and 1939, the knowledge that the student body of American universities was wholeheartedly antagonistic to the philosophy of Fascism, whether in its German or in its Italian form, was to me one of the strongest proofs that none of the sporadic manifestations of that doctrine in America had taken deep root in the mental climate of the United States.

I felt that confidence most securely in the winter and spring after Munich, when I was on leave of absence from my own university in the United States. I travelled across the continent. Whether in Columbia or

Harvard in the East, whether in Indiana or Illinois in the Middle West, whether in Washington or California on the Pacific coast, the general atmosphere among the students was broadly identical. It was felt that Munich was a disaster to freedom and democracy. It was felt that Britain had dishonoured itself in being an accomplice in the annihilation of Czecho-Slovakia. It was felt that it was the duty of any nation which claimed to express the common interests of civilisation to take a determined stand against the aggressive tyranny of Hitler and Mussolini. Especially was this felt with passion by students of Left opinions. They emphasised, everywhere, the difference between the British attitude of "appeasement" to the Fascist dictators, and the Soviet insistence on the need of a firm stand against them. They asked—I felt that they were entitled to ask—whether something had gone wrong with the British people that it did not insist to the Chamberlain Government upon the plain fact that each "dose" of "appeasement" merely stimulated the arrogance and the appetite of the Dictators. I found that, everywhere, there was sympathy with the hostility of the British Labour Party to the Chamberlain policy. Communists, in particular, urged upon me the importance of an alliance between the nations opposed to the Dictators; and it was their view that those in Britain who realised the menace of Hitlerism, like Mr. Churchill, for instance, should, despite all ultimate differences, combine their forces to make headway against the more urgent danger.

I was in full sympathy with these views. I knew that it is always perilous to embark upon the grim path of war. But I felt that the objectives Hitler and Mussolini had in view were incompatible with peace. I was convinced that nothing but a direct challenge would end their advance; and I was certain that, where they planted their feet, there all the main elements of civilised living were destroyed. I could explain, I could not defend, the motives of the Chamberlain Government. I insisted, arousing sometimes a faint scepticism, but, I think, always a strong approval, that a time would come when public opinion in Britain would demand from its Government that it would fight rather than co-operate in the erosion of European freedom. No one, I add, was more clear that this was the international duty of a power like Great Britain than students who belonged to, or sympathised with, the Communist Party.

At long last, after the annihilation of Czecho-Slovakia on March 15, 1939, British public opinion, led by Mr. Churchill on the Right and by the Labour Party on the Left, compelled Mr. Chamberlain to set limits to the "appeasement" which was endurable. The guarantees to Poland, Rumania and Greece were, obviously, given in haste, and without that full understanding with the Soviet Union which should have been their logical prelude. I admit fully that the absence of that understanding was the outcome of profound prejudice against the Soviet Union on the part of the Chamberlain Government; prejudice, further, which was bound to arouse the suspicion in the Soviet mind either that Mr. Chamberlain hoped that the guarantees would switch Hitler's ambition to the possibilities of an attack upon the Soviet Union, or that their existence would compel Hitler to some accommodation he could accept. I do not know at what stage the minds of the rulers of the Soviet Union decided that their negotiations with the West offered less prospect of Soviet security than a treaty with Hitler; I understand fully why the attitude of the Chamberlain Government persuaded them that its prejudices against an understanding with Britain and France were too strong to be overcome. On a short-term view, the decision of the Soviet Union to safeguard itself against an attack by Hitler was, in the light of its situation, wholly intelligible. If "appeasement" was good enough for Mr. Chamberlain, it was obvious self-interest for Stalin and Molotoff. It gave them time to reinforce their strength. It safeguarded them against the danger that the full weight of the Nazi legions would be hurled immediately, as in 1914, against them. Their invasion of Finland was presently to display how deeply they felt that danger.

What, I think, they failed to understand was the temper of the British people. Once Mr. Chamberlain had been forced by public opinion to give his guarantees, no Government in Britain could have survived which sought to evade their implementation. That, I think, also, must have been clear to anyone who was in Britain in the five months before the outbreak of war; it is shown beyond a shadow of doubt by the debates in the House of Commons in the week which preceded its declaration. Grave as was the shock to the world when the German-Soviet agreement was suddenly announced—it was the obvious harbinger of conflict—it never deflected for one moment either the British people, or the parties of the Left, from their resolution to have done with "appeasement," even at the price of war. They felt that a life passed under its perpetual threat was unendurable; and their conviction was profound that no civilised progress was possible in a world which permitted Hitler and his allies continually to brandish this threat as a means of extending the authority of the Fascist powers. It must be added that, at this stage, if the Communist Party of Great Britain regretted that it fell to the Chamberlain Government to conduct the war, it had no doubt whatever of the rightness of the decision to fight. "To stand aside from this conflict," wrote Mr. Harry Pollitt early in September, 1939, "to contribute only revolutionary-sounding phrases while the Fascist beasts ride roughshod over Europe, would be a betrayal of everything our forbears have fought to achieve in the course of long years of struggle against capitalism." That was, I think, an almost universal opinion among British Socialists of every description; the small Independent Labour Party was the only organised Socialist body which was from the outset opposed to the war.

It is well known that, about a month after the outbreak of war, the British Communist Party, in conjunction with the other constituent parties of the Third International, reversed this attitude. Mr. Harry Pollitt was dismissed from his leadership of the party; and, under its new direction, a nation-wide campaign was organised to argue that, so far as Great Britain was concerned, this war was simply an "imperialist" war the continuance of which was contrary to the interests of the working class everywhere. It was insisted that the defeat of Poland (which by then had been divided between Hitler and the Soviet Union) ended any reason for its continuance; the duty of Socialists, it was argued, was to make peace with Hitlerite Germany. That attitude on the part of the British Communist Party was maintained with increasing emphasis until Hitler's attack on the Soviet Union on June 22, 1941. What exactly the Communists meant by "peace" and what motives underlay their attitude they never succeeded in making clear even to their friends.

It was about this time that letters from the United States and articles in American journals began to make it clear that the issues of the war profoundly divided American student opinion. Some of it accepted the frank Communist view that the war was simply an "imperialist" war which working-class action must end at the earliest opportunity. Others argued that the war was a purely European affair, and a "phony" war at that; the duty of Americans was to stand aside from it and deal with their own grave social problems. Others, again, insisted that a negotiated peace was the only way to prevent that rising tide of national hatreds which, largely because of the weight of American intervention, had led to the disillusionment of 1919 and the inter-war years. The improbability was urged of a Government like the British measuring up to the implications of the war. All of this was exacerbated, first, by the depth of the divisions over the Soviet attack on Finland, and the belief, so long and so ardently proclaimed by the Communists, that it was the prelude to an attack, dreamed of for a generation by reactionary capitalism, against the Soviet Union—a policy, so the *New Masses* always insisted, of a British accommodation with Hitler at the expense of Moscow. After the fall of France, it was exacerbated again by the depth of the conviction among many students that modern war fascises the nation which embarks upon it; Mr. Kennedy and the Communists joined hands, though for very different reasons, to proclaim that British democracy was "finished." The way for America to retain its democracy was to practise, both in mind and deed, wholehearted aloofness from the conflict.

I heard in letters from friends of how widespread these attitudes were on the American campus. By some, they were regarded with despair or indignation. They were the outcome, I was told, of a blindness to ideals on the part of students which augured ill for the future of American democracy. Others were dismayed at what they termed the "cynicism" of students; it was tragic that they could remain unmoved by the spectacle of freedom in danger. One eminent university figure told me that their cause was the "poison of Marxism" which had made masses of students indifferent to any questions save those of power. Mr. McLeish, it will be remembered, thought that students had read the wrong books; it was Hemingway, Remarque and their like whose insidious influence had warped their clarity of vision. To Professor Mortimer Adler the situation was the outcome of a general decay of values which could only be arrested by a return to the philosophy of St. Thomas Aquinas.

I confess that none of these explanations moved me at all seriously. Though it is, through the war, almost two years since I was last in the United States, I could not believe that the mind of the American student was profoundly changed in the interval. I could believe that the immensity of the issues at stake brought with it a natural confusion. I could believe, also, that men and women to whom humanism was important were appalled at the prospect of a war involvement in which might bring the risks of a new age like the nineteen-twenties with its ardent hopes and massive disillusions. But my own knowledge of the American student convinces me that at no period in my own lifetime has he been so receptive to the call of great ideas when greatly stated. More than this. So far from the "poison of Marxism" being responsible for confusion of thought, profoundly as I differ from them, I know that there are no students in American colleges more devoted to the service of an idea, or more self-sacrificing in activity on its behalf, than members of the Communist Party. I think they set the ideas in wrong perspective; and much of the activity it evokes from them seems to me wrong as procedure and futile as objective. But if I had to find a comparison for their devotion, I should have to go back to the first missionaries of the Quaker gospel, who set out to preach their faith in a world as difficult and confused as our own, three hundred years ago.

The confusion of mind among American students has, I believe, one major and one minor cause. The major cause is the simple fact that the crisis in our civilisation is, naturally enough, reflected in the universities; it would be astonishing if this were not the case. The divisions among them are no more remarkable than the divisions in the Congress of the United States, which reflect the same crisis. They are the divisions which existed among the British students and in the Parliament of Great Britain until they were effaced by the profound realisation that our very existence as a free people was at stake in this war. The geographical position of the United States is, by itself, sufficient to account for what detachment there is from the impact of Nazism. It is necessary, it has been necessary here, for men to see the price it exacts for its expansion before they can measure with sober accuracy the magnitude of its threat to civilisation. One has only to remember how tragically the small European peoples clung to the fiction of their neutrality to grasp the compulsion which weighs on students three thousand miles away from the conflict to rationalise their fear of being sacrificed to its inexorable demands.

The minor cause is more subtle, but it is, I believe, none the less real for that. American universities have suffered, for at any rate half a century, from the excessive domination of wealth over their activities. To evade the incidents involved in that domination they have frowned upon those teachers who answered the challenge of our civilisation in an unorthodox way. In the social sciences, where, in this period, the real battle of doctrine has been fought, the governing bodies of universities have sought, at all costs, either for "safe" professors, or for those the burden of whose teaching did not arouse undue scepticism about the foundations of the American commonwealth. The result, in a considerable degree, has been the banishment from the class-room of fundamental discussion of the living issues of the day; or where, above all arrestingly, the discussion became fundamental, a presidential frown was the main reward which greeted the teachers who promoted it. Those who make it difficult for men like Veblen and Charles Beard to serve a university are not entitled to surprise if the mind of the student is confused about essential values. Understanding comes to those only who have been permitted to examine without penalty the clash of ideas in the market-place. If there free examination is denied, the price is always paid in an easy acceptance of naïve dogma. The student who is not permitted to think of the university as a temple of truth is the most certain victim of extreme philosophies. For not having been trained to the examination of all assumptions, he is too often helpless before any creed which offers him a confident pattern of the universe about him.

The students of this generation, on any showing, have been born into a difficult and complex world. The old certainties are gone; the old values are in the melting-pot; religious faith no longer offers a secure rock upon which they might lay their feet. In such a mental climate, the duty of the universities was boldly to examine the problems of the time. For them, it ought not to have mattered whether the teacher was Communist or Conservative so long, first, as he was honest in his convictions, and so long, second, as he had the gift of making the student find his way to the heart of his problems. It was, of course, important that the student should be exposed to the clash of doctrine; wisdom is born of the compulsion to choose freely in the light of mighty opposites. But, in general, the power to make such a choice was rare. The compulsion upon universities to play for safety in discussion of social doctrine was profound; it was often difficult to discover from professors' lectures, or from their books, what they believed, if, indeed, they believed anything. Year after year the American Association of University Professors was compelled to enquire into dismissals for unorthodox views. Even more important was that pre-natal control on the expression of radical ideas which comes from the knowledge that it is a hindrance to promotion.

Now the student mind, from its very nature, is interested in unorthodox ideas. It is a young mind, exercising, for the first time, the joy of the intellectual chase. It is in its first period of eager escape from the fetters of the formal discipline of school. Naturally enough, whatever is unconventional is by that very reason arresting to it; naturally enough, also, whatever is forbidden or frowned upon is by it the more eagerly explored. To youth, in its ardour, achievement is easy, action important, for its own sake, challenge of the accepted normal; it takes seven or eight years in an American university to transform the excited youth who, for the first time, is learning to hew principle from the raw facts into the average sober Doctor of Philosophy who has so largely abandoned the hope of significant generalisation. To confront minds of this temper, eager, vivid, generous, with a denial that all matters are open to investigation—the sole principle, in any case, upon which the existence of universities can be justified—is to invite exactly the scepticism of traditional values the prohibition is intended to prevent.

I believe, therefore, that American universities have a certain responsibility for that mental climate among the student body which persuades them to aloofness from that outlook in the war against Hitler which to us in Britain seems, with such overwhelming emphasis, inescapable. The debate on values which ought, over all these years, to have been a central part of the teacher's task in the lecture room has not taken place there; it is not surprising that it has been supplied from elsewhere, not as doctrine to be analysed, but as activity to be embraced. If the evaluation of institutions is replaced by the mere description of institutions; if one-time rebels like Hobbes and Rousseau can be examined as classical texts, while the examination, in the same spirit, of Marx and Lenin is attended with danger to the examiner; if the American and French Revolutions can be studied as though they had no effective relation to the Russian Revolution; if Pareto is deemed respectable and the *Communist Manifesto* dangerous; the result is to deprive the student, just at the period when he most burns to interpret, even to change, the universe, of the sense that he is being significantly taught. Since that deprivation means that the abler the student, the more profound is the frustration he will suffer, he is certain to make his protest; and the most natural form his protest will take, in an institution which, while emphasising publicly its zeal for freedom in ideas, is privately creating safeguards against its consequences, is rejection of the values the university appears to embody. The governing bodies of the American college have still, by and large, to learn the great lesson that students attain a wise balance in matters of social constitution in proportion to the profundity of doctrinal freedom they experience.

That, I think, needs to be said. But when it is said, I confess to real dismay at the thought that any significant proportion of American students is doubtful about the imperative need for a British victory in this war. The alternatives to this victory seem to me, as a British Socialist of the Left, fraught with disastrous consequences. The one alternative is a peace of accommodation with Hitler. The other alternative is our defeat by Hitler. The second, as I know, is desired by no one in any American university of which I have knowledge. It would mean, so clearly, the fall of night over Europe, and the rapid certainty of an American war with Hitler, that none of those even most suspicious of British motives and policy desires it. That defeat would mean the end of democracy and freedom in the old world. It would mean that Hitler would swiftly attain a position in which he could mobilise the resources of an enslaved Europe to challenge, in what order he chose, the remaining peoples not subject to his power. And its impact on the Far East would, almost certainly, compel the surrender of China to the evil aggression of Japan. That victory means a nightmare world from which, for any period this generation needs to foresee, the hope of security and ordered progress would be decisively banished. Those of us, above all, who look forward to a new and better social order are bound to remember the significant words of Mao Tse Tung, the Chinese Socialist leader. "We cannot even speak of Socialism," he said, "if we are robbed of a country in which to practise it."

I desire, therefore, to consider from a number of different angles why, to a British Socialist, the victory of Great Britain is the necessary pre-condition of a possible Socialist future. I desire to explain to American students why I support the Churchill Government and think it urgent, as a Socialist, to take all the risks—I know there are risks—involved in its support. I want to convince the American student, who is sceptical, if I can, that none of the easy slogans by which he has been persuaded to regard our effort with suspicion is justified. That the foundations of this war are laid in the implications of capitalism in its imperialist phase I do not deny; I want to persuade him that this is not, nevertheless, an imperialist war of the classic type against which Lenin inveighed. I want, further, to persuade him, if I can, that if we Socialists in Britain accepted what the Communists accepted until June 22, 1941—the policy of revolutionary defeatism—we should quite certainly ensure a Hitler victory. I want to persuade him, if I can, also, that the argument that it makes little difference to the British worker whether he is governed by Mr. Churchill or governed by Herr Hitler is as ignorant as it is absurd. I want to make it clear, moreover, that the policy of peace without victory—the policy in substance recommended by Communists before the fall of France—is not only impossible on any terms which a self-respecting Socialist could accept, but is, in the nature of the conditions we confront, merely an invitation to a renewal of the present conflict at a later stage. If I can do this, it seems to me that there emerges the ground for his acceptance of the argument which we British Socialists accept—the necessity of a Europe freed from the authority of either Hitler or Mussolini.

Two other things I must say with emphasis. My plea

that the American student should recognise the need of a British victory is not a plea for direct American participation in this war. It is, indeed, a plea for the continuance of that massive material aid which the generous understanding of the President and Congress of the United States, backed, as I believe, by the overwhelming support of the American people, have made available to us in the Lease and Lend Act. Faced as we are by a Germany which has not only been re-arming for eight years, but now draws upon the resources of half a continent, that material aid is an essential condition of our victory. But I believe Mr. Churchill to have been right when he said that we do not need American man-power for victory. With what decisions the United States may be confronted by the action of Hitler or his associates I do not, of course, know. But, on the assumption that they are not guilty of the folly of provoking the United States to an unavoidable belligerency, I believe it is better for the world that, on the plane of action, American intervention should be limited to the kind of material aid we are now receiving, than that Americans should send their youth to die on the European battlefield. It is, I think, within our power to defeat Hitler and Mussolini without that sacrifice.

The other thing it is important for me to emphasise is that I am not for one moment arguing that the victory of Britain means the inevitability of a Socialist order in this country, or in Europe generally. I think it could mean that; I hope it will mean that. But, in the first instance, I agree at once that a British victory will mean no more than the destruction of the two dictators whose aggressions have been the vital occasion of this war. I do not think it is easy to exaggerate the importance of that destruction. Of itself, it will lift the shadow of terror from the lives of one-quarter of a billion human beings. Of itself, it will re-establish all over the world, not least in the United States itself, that respect for democratic procedures and for the rule of law which are vital both to international peace and to that security which gives to Reason its hold over the minds of men. To us who have lived now grim days with the victims of Nazi barbarism from half the countries of Europe, and have passed nights of terror while Hitler's aeroplanes deliberately bombed civilian objectives in city and in countryside, this is no light thing. Americans who have not been machine-gunned in a train, or crouched in an air-raid shelter while the bombs crashed mercilessly down for the long hours of darkness, cannot perhaps measure this emancipation in the same terms or with the same intensity as we do. I will only say that, quite literally, the very hope of it is like stepping out of blackness into light.

Of itself, I do not claim that victory will bring Socialism; I only say that, without victory, all the necessary conditions for the establishment of Socialism are absent. The institutions, political, economic, social, through which it may come are destroyed in every country which comes under Hitler's heel; the Gestapo executes or imprisons all the men and women ready to lay their hands to the building of Socialism. I do not think I need argue this to any American student who has followed with any closeness the fate of France in defeat. There was much that was unedifying and corrupt in the France of the Third Republic. Is there any American to deny that, whatever its sins, it was, by comparison with the France of Vichy, a great commonwealth, in which the ordinary man had not yet been deprived of that hope which gives life meaning? Or is there, either, any American student who will deny that there is no hope, at least in our time, for the revival of a free and democratic France save in the defeat of Hitler? What is true of France, so much the most tragic of the nations because the greatness of her fall was so complete, is true of all the nations whom Hitler has conquered. No people dares to hope save upon the basis of a British victory. That victory is, at the least, the road to national emancipation from a slavery as profound as any an Oriental despot has imposed. That national emancipation at least leaves in being the institutions, and the men and women, through whose faith and energy and devotion the democratic Socialist commonwealth may be built. And, granted the temper of at least my own people, I believe the grounds for the conviction that we shall seek to build a society whose freedom is deeply rooted in social and economic equality are more strong than at any previous time. I do not say that victory makes such a society inevitable; there are no inevitabilities in history. I say only that, with victory, a real opportunity is there, that, without it, Europe will become a society of slave nations geared to the relentless purpose of the Nazi tyrant. The American student must realise that this is not idle rhetoric. It has happened to Poland and Czecho-Slovakia; it is happening to France; in somewhat less intensity it is happening to Holland and Belgium and Norway. We are determined upon victory because, first, we would rather die than accept that fate, and because, second, in victory we can release the sister-nations of Europe from its ugly tragedies.

This is what, if I can, I want to make the American student understand. I do not address my argument to students of the Left alone; though, naturally, my own preconceptions will make it more acceptable to them. But I am concerned to persuade the average American student that the character of this war makes it evident that the defeat of Hitlerism is part of the necessary strategy of American defence; that, unless that defeat be a total one, the whole of the world is condemned to an insecurity which jeopardises civilised living for any period of which our generation need take account. We are seeking to resist a conqueror who, as each new revelation of his ambitions has made plain, aims at nothing less than world dominion. His victory would be the end of free co-operation. It would mean the deliberate subjection of every people to the satisfaction of his lust for power.

If it is said that we in Britain were slow to form this conclusion; that we took no action over Japanese aggression in 1932; that we sacrificed Spain and Austria, Abyssinia and Czecho-Slovakia, to a narrow self-interest, I admit the impeachment that challenge contains. It is true that, like the Soviet Union, we sought to come to terms with this relentless gangster; it is true, also, that, like the Soviet Union, we have paid grimly for our mistake. We have learned from experience that the fate of all free nations is, under modern conditions, interdependent; that if we are careless, as we were careless, of the liberties of others, we throw our own in jeopardy. It is this which has made it possible for Mr. Churchill and the British Labour Party to find ends in common which, until victory comes, outweighs their differences. It is this, also—could anything be more significant?—which made Mr. Churchill see at once in the German invasion of Russia a blow aimed at Great Britain which gave us and the citizens of the Soviet Union a common cause. I should agree that, in the inter-war years, the politics of European diplomacy were such as, on a superficial view, to encourage the American sense that freedom from "entangling alliances" was the part of wisdom. I do not think it can be seriously argued that this is the case to-day.

For two reasons. No American can soberly believe that a Europe, including Russia, which lay under Hitler's heel could leave the United States indifferent to its fate. It is evident that the collapse of Europe would bring into immediate jeopardy the highest interests of the American continent, above all those spiritual values which have made American influence on the world significant. A defeated Europe means not only a permanently militarised America, but, at some stage, which Hitler, and not America will choose, it means an America at war in much the same circumstances as we confront to-day. For a victorious Hitler dare not disarm; he could not afford the risk of revenge from those he would have enslaved. He dare not even halt in his advance; for he could not, if he halted, continue to control his subjects for the purposes he embodies. Just as we have awakened to the realisation that his defeat is the price of our freedom, so Americans have to recognise that our victory is the price of their security. Their interest in it is immediate and direct and tangible. It is being fought for to-day by the armed forces of Britain and the Soviet Union.

The other reason is one of which an Englishman speaks with some self-consciousness, but of which, at this hour, he is, I think, entitled to speak. No one who has seen Britain at war, above all since the fall of France, can doubt that there has taken place something like a spiritual regeneration of her people. The qualities which have enabled them to strive against fearful odds, the courage, the resolution, the self-sacrifice and the self-discipline of a free people, these, I say with pride and confidence, have been an example to the world. It is an example impossible after shattering defeat to any people to whom the traditions of liberty and self-government were not of vital importance. It is an example built, above all, on the inner and ultimate determination of the British working class to remain the unfettered master of its own destiny. Can any American student seriously and honestly believe that workers who have passed through the fires of tyranny from abroad will sit down meekly to accept the imposition of tyranny from at home? Can he not understand that the working class of this country grows in intellectual comprehension of its problems as suffering has made it grow in moral stature? Can he believe that a great party like the British Labour Party, having battled for years against Nazi tyranny and for friendship with the Soviet Union, is really so stupid or so dishonest as to assist in the betrayal of the class from whose experience it was born and by whose overwhelming will it is a full partner in the Churchill Government?

At least I may ask from the American student a patient examination of the argument by which, as a Socialist, I defend the choice I have made. If he rejects the argument, I ask him to show in what manner the Nazi defeat may be achieved within a period that has meaning for our generation. If he accepts it, I ask him to undertake the task of convincing his fellow-students of the need fully to associate American energies with the grave tasks that lie ahead of us upon the terms that the President and Congress of the United States are prepared to approve. I assume that, whatever our differences, we share the common assumption that Hitlerism, in all its forms, is the supreme menace to what is worthy in our civilisation. For if we did not argue from that assumption, we could not, any longer, think as free men.

Two

We are told that this is an imperialist war; its central issue, it is insisted, is merely whether the workers of the world are to be exploited under British capitalism or under German. It matters nothing, we are to assume, whether it is exploitation by the one or by the other.

The business of a Socialist is to examine each historical situation as it arises in order to distinguish between its progressive and reactionary elements; and it is his duty to support the one and to attack the other. To stand apart from those situations is to declare that they have no meaning for Socialism.

For war, clearly enough, and especially upon its present scale, is so revolutionary an event in the life of a people that it is sheer futility to look upon it as no more than a conflict between warring factions of the bourgeoisie with which Socialists need have no concern. That view, I suggest, is based upon a wholly illegitimate analogy with the war of 1914. Russia apart, that struggle was between two groups of states the social structure of which was basically similar in nature. From the angle of Socialists, the defeat of either group presented a situation implicit with revolutionary possibilities. And, from that angle, it was no easy matter for Socialists to make the distinction between progressive and reactionary elements that is fundamental. That was even more the case because the Franco-British alliance with Czarist Russia might, under other circumstances, have given the evil régime of Nicholas II a lease of continued life.

The difference between the war of 1914 and the present war is, for Socialists, fundamental. It is the difference between the habits and implications of British imperialism, on the one hand, and those of Hitlerite imperialism on the other. Socialists do not need either to deny or to forget what is evil and ugly in the first, above all in India; but they need constantly to remember the inescapable characteristics of the second. For British imperialism has passed its phase of expansion and aggression; Hitlerite imperialism is seeking to enter upon it. The effect of the war upon British imperialism will be to develop still further those centrifugal and disintegrating tendencies which have already won for the Dominions the position of virtually independent states, and are rapidly pushing India in the same direction. The effect on Hitlerite Germany of a victorious war would be, clearly, to consolidate the power of a new and vigorous imperialism, at the beginning of its expansion, and using methods of governance far more oppressive than those of contemporary Britain.

I take British India as a crucial case. I do not for one moment deny the grave inadequacies of British rule there. But even those inadequacies leave to the Indian people far more real opportunities for advancing their national freedom than is the case with those nations which have been brought under the domination of Hitlerite Germany. The reason for this is simple. British imperialism has been essentially a capital-exporting imperialism. British investors, in their search for higher profits, have industrialised increasingly the colonies under their control; by so doing they have prepared there the social forces (including the class relations) which make possible that growth of the economic and political consciousness of which emancipation is the logical outcome.

But Hitlerite imperialism is imperialism of a new type. It is, in the first place, a deliberate subjugation of the territories it conquers to the totalitarian economy of Germany. Its aim prohibits the economic development of the territories it occupies in such fashion as to develop their people also. On the contrary, it seeks to exploit their resources, especially in raw materials and agriculture, while avoiding the consequences of industrialisation. Its colonists, both on the human and on the material side, are to be the peons of a conquering race. This is seen clearly in the treatment by Germany of the conquered peoples in Poland and Czecho-Slovakia. Not only are they the legal inferiors of Germans. Not only are their lands and possessions confiscated without compensation for the benefit of German settlers. The segregation of subject-peoples to special areas (for example, the Jews in the Lublin reserve) is also a feature of the German system. Their cultural life is ruthlessly destroyed. They are forbidden to unite for political protection or economic defence. The worst features of slavery, the more tragic, because they are imposed on men and women who have known freedom, are characteristic of Hitlerite imperialism. It is a barbarism such as Europe has not known since the worst excesses of the Thirty Years' War.

The conclusion, surely, for Socialists, is vital. It is

that, although the war is a conflict between two imperialist systems, on the one side Great Britain represents an imperialism the very nature of which gives hope of progressive development, while that of Hitlerite Germany represents, by its end and its procedures, repression of the most reactionary kind. The inner essence of Nazism, as Socialists have long insisted, is the attainment of power by conquest; and to maintain and consolidate its conquests when won it is compelled to impose slavery on those whom it conquers. For it has, otherwise, no hope of maintaining its hold upon its victims. Their economy, their organisation, even their ideas, must be set in the perspective of the Gestapo and the concentration camp. The boasted "new order" of Hitler is a grim mercantilism in which all Europe is forcibly transformed into a vast prison colony, with the prisoners driven, as Dr. Ley has said, to "sweat blood" for their German masters.

Nor is that all. Socialists have not only to distinguish between these two types of imperialism. They have also to seek to measure the world impact of a Hitler victory. It means, now, not only the fall of Britain and the Soviet Union. It means the devotion of the immense resources Hitler would control to the safeguarding of the power so acquired from American threat. And since the method used to safeguard himself by Hitler is that not of conciliation, but of challenge, his victory means for the United States an experience, first, of directly stimulated internal disunity, and then, when he deemed the moment ripe, of aggressive attack. He would use to these ends all the ugly anti-democratic forces which proliferate over the American continent. He would stir up all the divisive forces so patently at his disposal there. The perspectives opened to him and to the United States by his victory literally beggar the imagination as one begins to scan their implications.

It is too easy to reply, as men like Colonel Lindbergh would doubtless reply, that a strongly-armed America need have no fear of the outcome. To that view there are many answers. There is the answer, first, that a Europe reorganised under Hitler for the purposes of war has at its disposal resources vast enough to make easy prophecies of American victory vain and empty assertions. There is the answer, second, that the kind of historical epoch into which, under these circumstances, America would move would have about it a stark brutality incompatible with the way of life most Americans find rational and acceptable. It might satisfy those who, like Colonel Lindbergh and his main associates, think little of the common man and his search for an individual road to happiness. It might give contentment to those against whose principles the experimental America of the last ten years has been nothing so much as a magistral protest. It would be an epoch without meaning for Americans to whom the faith of Jefferson and the ideals of Lincoln retain their significance. For it would be bound to submerge the individuality of the common man before the unceasing demands of a vast Leviathan concerned only to organise power and yet more power. It would be a time of which the central characteristic was the deployment of collective strength at the expense of private freedom. It would put in hazard every hope of the development of those private virtues which make life lovely, since its insecurity would mean that only man's public context would have significance. The defeat, in a word, of Britain and the Soviet Union would be the end of that America to which Washington and his colleagues gave birth. And even if, after great sacrifice, the new America triumphed, it would be long before its possibilities were recovered, as they now exist, for the common man.

The defeat of Hitlerite Germany, on the other hand, would be the signal for the release of renovating and revolutionary forces. That would mean not only the recovery, over a vast area, of European freedom from a slavery which every independent observer has found hateful. It may mean, also, the growth of social forces able to take a great step forward in the emancipation of mankind from the tyranny of things. Modern war, on the scale of this war, is essentially revolutionary in its incidence. It compels new habits by the ruthlessness of its demands. It is a ceaseless experiment in methods of organisation which end, once and for all, the economic anarchy of a planless world. There is at least the prospect before of us of a new and more profound 1848, a realisation, by the working-class forces, and of elements beyond their ranks, of the need to give a new and wider meaning to liberty and equality. That prospect began to emerge during the last war. It was to prevent the realisation of its consequences that Hitler was assisted to power in Germany, as Mussolini had been in Italy, by the Army and the big industrialists of Germany; and it was because only that realisation could have saved France that Pétain and Weygand surrendered. I do not claim that a victory of Britain and the Soviet Union means the triumph of a new and better social order in Europe; after the disillusion of 1919 it would be folly to make any such claim. But I do claim that such a victory means at least the possibility of carrying to completion those principles which proved premature in 1848, and that, without it, there is no hope, in our lifetime, for the workers of Europe and America.

If to this argument the American student replies that he is not interested in such a revolution, there are, I think, two replies. The first is the simple one that he then aligns himself with the anti-democratic forces; there are no neutrals in the struggle upon which we are engaged. He so aligns himself because in this war it is necessary to understand that the strength of the armed forces each side can organise and equip is built upon their power to appeal to the moral energy and resolution of the workers in field and factory. And that power, in the long run, is a function of the dynamic each side can make available. Europe cannot deny Hitler with Hitler's ideology; it can deny him only by relying upon ideas which prove its inadequacy for the end it has set before itself. And to prove that inadequacy it is compelled to give hope and exhilaration to the populations it serves. This it can only do by striving to prove to them forthrightly its power to offer mankind a better fate than Hitler offers. As soon as the conditions of that fate are examined they involve changes in social relationships which go back, in their implications, to the frustrated hopes of 1848. They depend, that is, upon an extension of the frontiers of democracy. They mean that men have access to security and opportunity, that we remake the categories of authority which deny them that access. Those who declare that they are uninterested in this remaking have no alternative, in fact, but the acceptance of some such social framework as Hitler seeks to impose. For we cannot at once defeat him and stereotype society as it was on September 3, 1939; that Europe, on any showing, belongs now to the lumber-room of history. Our only problems are whether we are to go forward or backward, and the procedure of our movement. And, if we are to go forward, there is no other fundamental way of change than by a remaking of social relationships. Either we extend or we contract the frontiers of democracy. There is no middle way.

The second answer is not less important. The student who insists that he is not interested in such a revolution is saying not merely that he is not interested in Europe, but, just as vitally, that he is not interested in the American future. For on any profound view, the deeper causes of the European crisis are at work, if with retarded effect, in the United States. Mass unemployment; distressed areas; the maladjustment of purchasing power to productive capacity; the consequent need for foreign markets; the urgency of armed power to assure access to them; on the economic side all the phenomena which led to war in Europe have reality in America. There is there the same decay of traditional values, the same fervent literature of protest, the same sense, in youth, of a denial of opportunity, the same emergence—always characteristic of an age of crisis—of extremist philosophies and of the contempt for reason. What Mr. Wells has so aptly termed the "raucous voices"—Huey Long, Father Coughlin, McWilliams, Townsend—can be heard in America hardly less clearly than in Europe. The American student is at the parting of the ways. He has to choose; and he has to choose in the realisation that to refuse to choose is itself a significant choice.

Three

THERE are, I am told, American students who have argued that, from the workers' angle, it makes little difference whether Mr. Churchill or Herr Hitler is the victor in this war. No doubt they are fewer in number than they were before Hitler's assault on the Soviet Union. But I frankly confess that I do not understand this argument, the more so because it has so largely come from that source of opinion which, before the war, was urging the establishment of a Popular Front in which Mr. Churchill was to have been a pivotal figure. It was, in any case, based upon premisses which never had any relation to the realities we confront.

I do not, of course, forget that Mr. Churchill has been among the most formidable opponents the British Labour movement has known in the last generation. Equally, I realise that the kind of world he seeks to establish is not a world built upon principles for which Socialists of any complexion can stand. I know that there are indefensible acts in his record: the organisation of the attack on the Soviet Union after 1917, his position in the General Strike, his attitude in 1931. But to argue from these that the leadership of Mr. Churchill in the British war effort ought to mean a refusal on the part of Socialists to support him seems to me to start from the wrong premisses to reach the wrong conclusions.

Ever since Hitler came to power in Germany Mr. Churchill has been outstanding among those who recognised the dangers he represented. He was the enemy of appeasement; he was the outstanding critic of Munich; he was a foremost advocate, as all his speeches since 1933 have made manifest, of understanding with the Soviet Union. For us in Britain, he has come to symbolise, as much as any man, the determination of my fellow-countrymen not to yield to the Nazi dictatorship. The audacity and resolution he has brought to the war effort have steeled the hearts of British citizens in a way that no one can even begin to understand who has not felt at first-hand the inspiration of his leadership.

That leadership, in the context I am discussing, raises, clearly, two questions. The first is whether a British citizen, under the Government over which he presides, faces a future broadly akin to that which he would confront if Hitler were in power in this country. The second is whether a victory won under Mr. Churchill as Prime Minister deprives the Labour Movement of hopes it would otherwise possess.

Let me say at once that if this war could be won by a British Government either wholly or predominantly Labour I should myself prefer that Government to the one over which Mr. Churchill presides. There is no prospect that I can see—for reasons I shall examine later—of such a Government; and the business, therefore, of a British Socialist like myself is to deal with the objective situation, to use the instruments with which history has provided us, rather than to deal with historical might-have-beens, however attractive.

When the problem is set in these terms, I do not think the answer is in serious doubt. Mr. Churchill's power to remain Prime Minister during the war depends, disaster apart, upon his power to secure the assent of the Labour movement to his politics. That is the basis upon which his Government commands public confidence; and no one knows better than Mr. Churchill that it is the indispensable condition of his authority. So long as he possesses it, he can exact no sacrifices, he can make no decisions, of which the Labour Movement does not broadly approve. The conditions upon which the Labour Party entered his Government—that of a "full partnership"—have, so far, been amply observed; nor is there any reason, so far, to fear a departure from them.

I do not, of course, suggest that the policies of the Churchill Government have up to now altered in any basic or deliberate way the parallelogram of social forces in Britain. I do say that the historic defence mechanisms of the working class have, since he took office, not only at no point been jeopardised, but are stronger than they were when he became Prime Minister. The status of the trade unions is, by universal admission, higher than at any point in their history. The social services of the nation have, thanks largely to the effort of Labour Ministers, been notably strengthened and improved. The vitality of the classic civil liberties is incontestable; any impartial observer would, on this head, note, I think, an immense gain on the experiences of the war of 1914. The Communist Party makes great play with the introduction of industrial conscription into a number of vital war industries; and this is represented by its spokesmen as an assault upon the economic freedom of the worker. On this, however, there are two things to be said. Modern war depends in so great a degree on factory organisation that it renders obsolete and impracticable, as the Soviet Union as a planned society has found, the habits of a *laissez-faire* state. The surrender of freedom of movement by the worker is an essential condition of continuity of production. The question of freedom is not a function of the worker's right to change his job whenever he is so disposed; it is a question of whether, in the job he can do, he works under just conditions. Since, secondly, the full trade-union machinery of collective bargaining determines the basic character of those conditions, it is, I think, outrageous to suggest that the Churchill régime has worsened the status of the worker. The contrary is in fact the case.

The American student who compares the position of our people with those of the workers in Germany will know, if he has any sense of evidence, that those who speak of Mr. Churchill as, in fact, no less dangerous an enemy to Socialism than Herr Hitler, do not even lie honourably. For Mr. Churchill's authority is not the outcome of a dishonourable conspiracy implemented by organised terror; it is the response to the overwhelming demand of a free people whose democratic institutions have suffered no abridgement. And in that comparison lies the answer to the second of these questions. There is no escape for the German workers from Hitler save by way of bloody revolution. There is no hope of that revolution save as Hitler suffers complete military defeat. But Mr. Churchill's power depends upon the acceptance of his leadership by the House of Commons; and the shape of the House, in its turn, depends upon the free choice of the British people. If, when the war is over, Mr. Churchill's proposals for the reconstruction of this country do not meet with the approval of the Labour Party, the present National Government will be dissolved, and the voters will choose between them. No one supposes—no one, at least, in his senses—that Mr. Churchill will refuse to accept the verdict of the constituencies, destroy by decree, as Hitler has done, the trade unions, the co-operative societies, and the Labour and Communist Parties, and then proceed to govern Britain by a Tory Gestapo and its concentration camps. The fate of the British people, when this war has been won, will lie in the hands of the British people. To argue seriously that this makes no difference to the future of the workers is to put oneself out of court as an honest observer of the political scene. Mr. Churchill has made grave mistakes in his career; he has been guilty—witness the General Strike and India—of fantastic misjudgments; he has profound prejudices. But no one has ever supposed, and, on the record, no one has the right to suppose, that he will abandon parliamentary and constitutional methods in order to retain power.

It may be said that those who speak of Mr. Churchill as on the same plane as Hitler use his name in a symbolical sense only; they refer less to him than to those class-forces in Britain which, organised politically as the Conservative Party, would abandon the method of parliamentary democracy rather than surrender their privileges. On this, of course, there is much to be said. No one can predict the future with any confidence; it may be well that, in Britain as elsewhere, the governing class will rather fight than give way. But if that decision should come to be their choice, I am confident that their forces will not be led by Mr. Churchill. Steeped, in a career of nearly forty years, in the traditions of the House of Commons, I am certain that he does not think in those terms. It might well be, of course, that his refusal to do so would result in his being elbowed out of the leadership of the Conservative Party by some figure prepared for unconstitutional action. That, of course, is to admit how different is the plane of his thought from that of Hitler.

The truth is that, during the war-period, the only situation which could compel us to abandon our traditional political methods in Britain is that of shattering defeat; and we should then not be in a position to choose either the men or the methods by which our lives were directed. And, in those circumstances, looking at the countries Hitler has brought under his heel, I suspect that even the American student who thinks it makes no difference to the British worker whether he is governed by Mr. Churchill or Hitler would be tempted to revise his opinion. Certainly German students of the Left who, before 1933, thought that it mattered little whether Germany was ruled by Bruening or Hitler, if sadder, are wiser men.

They are, of course, wholly right who argue that, when the common objective of victory has been attained, Mr. Churchill and the Labour Party will have to travel along very different roads. They are even right who argue that his position, as leader of the Conservative Party, has led him to accept solutions and to protect interests hostile to the natural evolution of the democratic dynamic. But I think more vital than either of these is the proof Mr. Churchill gave, in his reaction to the Nazi attack on the Soviet Union, of his fitness for leadership in this war. He saw its inherent nature with sufficient profundity to be able to suppress the grave differences he symbolised before the great end that the British and Russian peoples have now in common. Those of us who had supported his leadership had no doubt that he would make this choice. It is less important that he made it for reasons other than those that a Socialist would advance than that he made it. Thereby, in an act of great statesmanship, he wiped out at a stroke the sorry history of Anglo-Russian relations since 1931. He made possible—I do not claim more—a new understanding between Great Britain and the Soviet Union when victory is won; and that new understanding, if it develops satisfactorily, is a fundamental key to enduring peace. The workers of Great Britain, certainly, will not forget in the post-war years the part that the Russian people has played in the overthrow of Nazi tyranny. And, frankly, it is the business of Socialists to remember that those of them who predicted that an attack on the Soviet Union by Hitler would serve Mr. Churchill as a pretext for "switching the war" profoundly miscalculated the forces that are in play. It is worth remembering that only two days before the Nazi attack on the Soviet Union the *New Masses* insisted upon its impossibility because its necessary prelude was an accommodation between Mr. Churchill and Hitler.

It is, of course, true that Mr. Churchill wages this war as a Conservative Nationalist concerned, above all, to maintain the freedom of Britain from Nazi domination. None of the elements which precipitated it present themselves to him in the terms in which they would be analysed by a Socialist. Nor does he understand the kind or the extent of the changes which, in the Socialist view, will be necessary to prevent any other power attempting in the future what Hitler has attempted. It is probable, too, that from a Socialistic angle, though Mr. Churchill has proved himself a great leader in war, the greatest we have known since Chatham, his insights are inadequate either to the peace or to the reconstruction that is required. The answer to these questions is Marx's famous answer that man does not make his history out of whole cloth. The problem for Socialists to-day is whether there is any available instrument of victory more likely to achieve it than Mr. Churchill; and it is the overwhelming opinion of organised Labour in Britain that there is no such instrument. That his presence at the helm will raise grave issues when victory is won I, as a Socialist, should not for a moment deny. But I share fully the views of my colleagues in the Labour Movement that we must face those issues when we come to them. It is, meanwhile, our task to ensure that Mr. Churchill presides over a victory. Our opportunities then will certainly be different from those we should confront were Hitler to shape our destiny as a people.

Four

AMERICAN students of the Left have been critical of the British effort because Mr. Churchill directs it, though, as I have said, since the Nazi assault on the Soviet Union their voices are likely to be fainter than in the past. Others are sceptical of our purpose because of their hatred of the Soviet Union and all its works. It is a tyranny; it is the foe of the Christian faith; it has been guilty of aggression against Finland and the three Baltic countries. To collaborate with the Soviet Union, we are told, is to risk the Bolshevisation of Europe. That would be a catastrophe hardly less gigantic than the victory of Hitler. Mr. Hoover, for instance, has been swift to announce that American aid to Russia destroys the hope of implementing the four freedoms which President Roosevelt has advocated so eloquently.

As a Democratic Socialist there is much in the policy of the Soviet Union that I cannot seek to defend. Most, indeed, of what I regard as indefensible is the outcome of a grim past the responsibility for which is only partly that of its present rulers. The legacy of economic and intellectual backwardness from the Czarist period; the tragic consequences of intervention and civil war; the environment of constant insecurity magnified, above all, by the diplomatic intrigues of the "appeasement" period—all these have their share in the definition of the present Russian régime. The follies and crimes of its present rulers have been very great. Yet, when the record is cast, there are, I think, two supreme matters to be taken into consideration. The first is the fact that, ever since its foundation, international peace has been the constant purpose of the Soviet Union; the second is the fact that, even in the ugly struggle for power within the Bolshevik party, the improvement of the condition of the people has been the constant aim its rulers have had in mind. There is no error more gigantic in our day than that which seeks to regard Bolshevism and Nazism as aspects of the same principle; their ends are poles asunder. Nazism cannot cease to be itself if it ceases to be an aggressive dictatorship; Bolshevism could become democratic without losing its informing and immanent principle. The supreme condition of that transformation is the achievement of external security; and the supreme condition of external security is the overthrow of Nazism. I do not say that the victory of Stalin over Hitler would mean the direct end of his personal dictatorship. I do say that it would create conditions out of which the emergence of Soviet democracy becomes a creative possibility. I do say, further, that there have been achievements in the Soviet Union, in the conquest of illiteracy, in the elevation of the backward peoples, in the improvement of the status of women, in the democratisation of the army, in the use of science as a social instrument, which surpass, in their quality, anything elsewhere achieved by modern nations in a comparable period of time.

In politics, as in nature, action and reaction are equal. Democratic freedom, as it has been known in Britain and the United States, is not a commodity that a nation can purchase like a loaf of bread on the market. It is the outcome of a civilisation the expansion of which has enabled its ruling class to have elbow-room which persuades them that the freedom of those they govern may be extended without risk to their privilege. That was not an experience enjoyed in Russia; and even in those countries which have enjoyed it, like the France of the Third Republic, the contraction of the elbow-room has made it grimly obvious that a ruling class prefers its privileges to the risks of a democracy built upon their surrender. In Germany and most of South-Eastern Europe the overthrow of Hitler and Mussolini means revolution; and it is possible that, for a period, that revolution will mean Bolshevisation. That prospect will, in my own judgment, alarm those only who are wedded at all costs to the maintenance of a privileged and unequal society.

For it is certain that régimes like those of pre-war Poland, of Hungary, of Rumania, exact, like those of Italy and Germany themselves, a revenge for the fate they have imposed upon the masses. The answer to Bolshevism is an answer that history has always given when long-felt grievances are at last released from suppression: it is whether those who are deprived of a power they have abused are willing to co-operate in attempting to build a just society. If they are determined to conspire and fight rather than give way, as in the Soviet Union, they make democracy impossible; for they provoke fear and insecurity, and these are the invariable parents of intolerance. If we seek a democratic Europe after the war, we must build the conditions in which alone democracy is possible—conditions which promise immediate well-being and future hope to the many and not to the few. Given victory, our power to promise these is very great. Our problem is whether we shall have the wisdom and magnanimity to give effect to that power.

The hostility of the Soviet Union to organised Christianity is set in the framework of similar considerations. That Lenin and his successors should have been profoundly suspicious of the Russian Church will only be unintelligible to those who are ignorant of its history; that they should have inhibited the free and full expression of religious belief will surprise those only who, first, do not recognise the complexity of the problem of Church and State, and are unaware, secondly, of the considerable part played by the Churches in organising directly or indirectly counter-revolution in the Soviet Union. I do not say for one moment that this justifies the intensity of Bolshevik repression of the Churches; but it explains far more of its character than is usually admitted. An Englishman is bound to remember the depth of fear aroused by the Roman Catholic Church in seventeenth-century England if he is to see this issue in an adequate context. And all of us are bound to remember the willingness of the Roman Catholic Church to co-operate in the suppression of freedom in Italy and Spain in return for power before we pass final judgment on the Russian experience.

If, of course, one takes the view that the Roman Church is the exclusive vehicle of salvation, and that its achievement is infinitely more important than happiness in this life, then clearly the values which Bolshevism seeks to express in social terms will seem irrelevant, and the spread of those values an unpardonable attack on the Church to be repelled at all costs.

For those who hold this view there can be no peace with the Soviet Union, and their purpose must be its destruction. But they are then left with the choice either, as in Italy and in Spain, of becoming the conscious allies of counter-revolution, or of becoming, what few Churches apart from the Society of Friends have ever sought consistently to be, the deliberate protagonists of social and economic changes profound enough to make possible a just society. It is not a choice about which Churches, as organisations, have hesitated often or long. Power rather than justice has been their main objective; and not a hundred pious Encyclicals compensate for the ardent support of one régime like that of Franco. There will be no peace between the Church and secular society so long as its adherents make temporal power the measure of their success. Nor will there be peace so long as a faith can insist that the persistence of poverty and its consequences is unimportant save in so far as they jeopardise the salvation of the rich.*

There was no justification for the Russian aggression against Finland. It was a piece of strategic imperialism which was rightly condemned not only by Great Britain and her Allies, but, also, by Democratic Socialists of all countries; and it was accompanied by a propaganda of hypocrisy which did immense damage as well as dishonour to its authors. That the aggression was the plain outcome of fear does not make it any the less aggression. It earned, indeed, a swift retribution in the zeal with which Finland associated itself with the

* On this see the powerful discussion by Professor Stebbing, *Ideals and Illusions* (1941), Chapter 1.

Nazi attack on Russia. What, however, is important in a long-run judgment is the zeal with which the enemies of the Soviet Union seized upon the aggression against Finland as a pretext for urging an attack upon a system they hated. They could watch unmoved the fate of Manchuria, of Austria, of Spain, of Czecho-Slovakia; they saw no pretext for a crusade in any of these. But immediately the Soviet Union committed this crime, they recognised it as crime and urged a holy war. Mr. Hoover, who had been uninterested even in the crucifixion of Czecho-Slovakia, was urgent in demanding the institution of relief for Finland. The war could hardly have demonstrated more clearly that men like Mr. Hoover had one standard of judgment for acts of the Soviet Union and another for Fascist aggressors. That was at least the proof that the fear of the Soviet Union of capitalist attack was grounded in reality. It does not excuse the aggression; but it does much to explain why it occurred.

The truth is that the attitude of Europe and America to the Russian Revolution has been as blind and as irrational as their attitude to the French Revolution a century and a half ago. In each case, they sought to build a *cordon sanitaire* about ideas because the rights of property were called into question. The American student who hates Communism will not destroy its influence by sympathising with this attitude. The answer to revolution is reform; a great idea can only be overcome by an idea still more great. I believe myself that this war will, if Hitler and Mussolini be defeated, be followed by something like universal European revolution; and I think it inevitable that much of its shape will be determined by the Soviet Union. I think, further, that the degree of Soviet influence will be a direct function of the tyranny and injustice that have preceded the outbreak of revolution. It will be easier to re-establish constitutional forms in, for example, Norway and Czecho-Slovakia, where the quality of government was high, than in Rumania or Germany, where it combined corruption with savagery. The gangster tradition does not beget the habit of democracy, simply because the gangster cannot be trusted to accommodate himself to the rule of law. And where, as with Italy since 1922, and Germany since 1933, every privileged interest fawned upon the gangsters until it was apparent that they threatened even those who were prepared to admire them, there the seed of Bolshevist ideas is being sown by the very men who fear its fruition. Those who have never demanded social justice for their neighbours must not be surprised if those neighbours suspect that they desire it only for themselves.

A simple analogy will perhaps make this clear. Mr. Henry Ford has been, throughout his life, the bitter enemy of trade unionism. To prevent its emergence in his factories he has employed hooligans and spies, has issued lying propaganda, and practised every evasion ingenuity could devise. He has even been willing to finance a man like Father Coughlin as the indirect instrument of his purpose. To every decent employer it has been an elementary principle that collective bargaining was the natural consequence of giant industry. Not until the combined influence of the American rearmament programme and the Wagner

Act threatened his access to profitable contracts from the Federal Government did Mr. Ford admit defeat. On the terms on which he sought to run his factories there was no possibility of just treatment for the individual worker. What Mr. Ford termed maintaining liberty of contract gave him, in fact, an imperial power over the lives of his workers which had in it many of the elements of slavery. Yet Mr. Ford could never be brought to understand that his own technique of violence bred a bitterness which was the inevitable parent of violence when any dispute arose in his factories. He resented any limitation upon the use of his authority; but if his property was ever endangered by his habits, he expected the whole force of the American Government to protect him. He was unresting in the assertions of his generosity as an employer who did not know the elementary habits of social justice.

I do not pretend to know what part the habits of Bolshevism will play in post-war Europe; I know only that it will be proportionate to the wrongs the masses have suffered. They do not turn to violence for its own sake; as even Burke saw, popular violence is the outcome of popular suffering. The conservative American student who fears that the defeat of Hitler will open the floodgates to Bolshevism has the elementary duty to see that the masses in their turn have something to conserve. A Europe that has hope and security will not risk either of these; that has never been the habit of men. But a Europe that has no prospect save despair will seek vengeance for its misery, and Bolshevism is the child of that despair.

From this angle, surely, it follows that the defeat of Hitler offers a greater prospect of constructive revolution than his victory, since the latter opens up no vista save that of further war and of rebellion among the peoples he has enslaved. The longer, moreover, that defeat is postponed, the more profound will be the misery of Europe, the greater the vengeance exacted as its price, the more fertile the ground for the reception of Bolshevist ideas. A conservative American, therefore, who desired to make as humane and brief as possible the transition to an ordered society from the horrors of this war can adopt no policy more fitting than that which speeds at its maximum the material aid necessary for Hitler's defeat, and, in its aftermath, the use of all the power and influence of the United States to prove that political democracy is substantial as well as formal. He must learn that the maintenance of constitutional government depends on the ability to know when men must abandon privileges that the masses deem unjustified. He may decide to maintain these privileges; but he must then remember that the condition of their maintenance is almost certain to be the necessity of abandoning constitutional government. And he must remember, further, in the light of both Italian and German experience, that in order to maintain them, he will be compelled to build alliances which deprive him of the power to control the purposes he has in view. The leader of violent revolution may, as John Morley said, tread a path of fire; it is certain that the leader of counter-revolution takes the path into the jungle. And where men once are set upon that path, there is no place for reason in their lives.

Most American students, I am told, are neither sympathisers with the Left nor with the Right. They want Britain to win, because they see the ugliness of the Nazi pattern. But they are above all eager that America should stay out of the war. They are for peace, not because they think time is wanted for preparation, but because they cannot imagine an evil worse than war. They think that the path the President has persuaded the American people to choose is bound to lead to American participation; and they look with dread to its consequences. They want America to stay confined in an icebox of neutrality. They fear what it may become once the shooting begins.

Frankly, I do not know if the accepted American policy will lead to war. That is not a matter upon which I think an Englishman has the right to pronounce. The evolving situation will produce certain states of fact upon which the Congress of the United States will have to take decisions. From our own angle, American belligerency has both advantages and disadvantages; I do not know which outweighs the other. The plain advantage is, above all, a psychological one, the impact upon the German and Italian peoples of the fact that their rulers have made you a fighting enemy. The disadvantage is twofold. There is the danger, first, that you may limit the flow of supplies to us and to the Soviet Union before the urgent problem of equipping your own forces. There is the danger, second, that an America roused by the passions of war may be less helpful, because less detached, in the building of peace than an America which has not directly experienced the meaning of war and can therefore take a more detached view of the way in which victory may be used.

Quite honestly, I cannot make up my mind on which side the balance of argument rests. Quite frankly, also, I am more interested in the motives which make Americans cling to the middle of the road than I am in the possible results of its actual belligerency. If I thought that we could not win without your participation, I should favour it. Now that we fight with the Soviet Union as our ally, I think we can win without the appearance of American armies in the field. It is therefore the motives of those who warn America against anything but a neutral policy which seem to me deserving of analysis.

The neutrals are, I believe, divisible into three groups. Two of them are curiously joined from persons of the Left and of the Right: Socialists like Norman Thomas, Liberals like President Hutchins and Senator La Follette, reactionary priests like Father Coughlin, and reactionary industrialists like Henry Ford and Generals Johnson and Wood. They are not, of course, for neutrality on the same grounds. The Left neutrals obviously believe that American democracy, unable to stand the strain of war, will go Fascist; and the Right neutrals are convinced that the outcome of war is a revolution in which "free enterprise," by which, in fact, they mean their privileges, will disappear. The Left neutrals are certain that, with war, Wall Street will put the President in its pocket. Free speech will disappear, the unions will be crushed, and all the gains, some of them, like the Wagner Act, immense gains, of the New Deal will be thrown in the discard. They think, in fact, that there can be no such thing as a "progressive" war. They cannot see that it has the power to create as well as to destroy. They see the dollar-a-year men in Washington using the authority of the state to protect their monopoly interests, and the common people reduced to a condition of peonage. They have no faith in the power of a liberated Europe to tackle the causes of war. They are still in the grip of the massive disillusions of the Harding-Coolidge epoch.

It is strange that their fears should be almost exactly paralleled by those of the Right neutrals. They are all in the mood of the men who sought to "appease" Hitler in the years before 1939. They think that war unleashes forces incompatible with the habits of capitalist America. They do not want to fight, or to risk the possibility of fighting, because they are convinced that war breeds revolution. They take the view that Mr. Chamberlain took until the occupation of Prague and the determination of British public opinion compelled him to recognise that there is a point at which further concession means shame. They are at one with Pétain and Darlan in thinking that some kind of accommodation can be arranged with Hitler, and that it is better to arrange it than to run the risk of releasing, as war may release, the dynamic of democracy. They reflect with fear upon the implications of American politics since 1933; they think those implications may be sharpened and deepened by a war fought to defeat the gangsters of monopoly-capitalism in Europe. For them, the entrance of the Soviet Union into the war, the strength of the trade-union forces symbolised by Mr. Bevin's presence in the British War Cabinet, are like the handwriting upon the wall. They are terrified of the collapse of an industrial empire the very nature of which is a contradiction of the American dream. If, somehow, they can get a compromise peace, and keep America safe from the disturbing winds of radical doctrine which begin to sweep over Europe, they are hopeful that the golden days of Harding and Coolidge may return.

I do not pretend to know which group of these curious partners is right. War creates opportunities; only the wisdom of men can take advantage of them. What is obviously certain is that both of them cannot be right. If American aid to Britain and the Soviet Union produces the results that Henry Ford so greatly fears, it cannot produce the results Mr. Hutchins apparently anticipates. My own view is very definitely that the trend of events is against Mr. Hutchins except in the case of a British defeat. "If we go to war," he is quoted as saying, "we cast away our opportunity and cancel our gains. For a generation, perhaps for a hundred years, we shall not be able to struggle back to where we were. In fact, the changes that total war will bring may mean that we shall never be able to struggle back. Education will cease. The effort to establish a democratic community will stop. We shall think no more of justice, the moral order, and the supremacy of human rights. We shall have hope no longer."

Those words of President Hutchins seem to me admirably to describe the condition of every country where Hitler has put his foot. They are ludicrously untrue of Britain which is waging total war. Of course it has meant deep suffering to wage it. But no one supposes that "our opportunity has been lost," or "our gains cancelled" or that they can be while there is power to go on fighting. We plan for a better system of education after victory. Even Conservatives like Mr. Churchill and Mr. Eden admit that our democracy must be made real. There is wider discussion of those things Mr. Hutchins believes we shall think of no more, wider discussion while the bombs fall on London and Plymouth, on Coventry and on Merseyside, than at any time during my life. What Mr. Hutchins describes is what Nazi Germany imposes. What he does not seem to understand is that what he describes comes only to those who refuse, if need be, to fight against its imposition. A defeated Britain might well be like his picture. A Britain which made some kind of patched-up peace with Hitler might well, in its uneasy insecurity, drift rapidly in that direction. There is no *a priori* reason to suppose that a victorious Britain will bear the least resemblance to his forecast. As to hope—what hope is there anywhere in the world for the sons of men save as we banish finally the nightmare of Hitlerism from our lives?

If Mr. Hutchins' picture is untrue of Britain in its hour of travail, it is even less likely to be true of an America that takes risks for freedom. If I may say so, I do not think that the Left neutrals, like him or Mr. Thomas, have any real understanding of the historic place of the Roosevelt epoch in American development. It is not a sudden or surprising thing. It is the lineal successor of the Progressive Movement, which, in its turn, was born of Bryanism; and this is linked with the popular revolts against economic oligarchy which reach back, through Andrew Jackson, to Jefferson and

John Taylor of Caroline in the early days of the Federation. I do not underestimate the power of American reaction; nor am I unaware of its ingenuity in utilising crises for its purposes. But the crisis it can most fully use is the one when a half-prepared America faces a triumphant Hitler with all the resources of Europe at his disposal. The Britain that nearly lost its power to choose was accommodating Britain, neutral Britain, appeasing Britain, the Britain of Baldwin and of Chamberlain, in whose image Mr. Hutchins and Mr. Thomas, like Mr. Ford and Colonel Lindbergh, would shape America. The Britain that retains its power to choose its way of life is the Britain that has challenged Hitlerism, that has relearned the ancient lesson that courage is the secret of freedom. For in taking up the challenge Hitler threw down it has undergone a spiritual renovation to which every independent observer bears witness. Compare the spirit of Mr. Churchill's speeches with the spirit of Marshal Pétain's. Set the faith in the people of the one against the ignoble defeatism of the other. Remember that the power of Mr. Churchill comes from the fact that a cause and an idea, the cause and the idea which are at the heart of the American dream, have electrified the people of Britain. What they are defending is their right to shape their own future, not to have it shaped for them. And no people can shape its own future that is not prepared to fight for it.

The Right neutrals know, far better than their Left colleagues, what they are about. They realise that an America in partnership with Liberal Europe will find ever more unanswerable the claims of the underprivileged.

They know that out of this association will grow a more deepening grasp of the economic possibilities of political power. They make no mistake when they infer that the defeat of Hitlerism is, in the long run, fatal to their authority. Their isolationism is, above all, an effort to stay the sweep of onc of those tidal waves in history from their own shores. If Hitler is victorious, they count either on some arrangement with him, which they believe would be fatal to the America of the New Deal, or, if a war becomes inevitable, they think they can wage it on their own terms. They suspect that his defeat means the break-through of ideas against which they have been fighting all their lives; and they are uneasily aware that they cannot set boundaries to those ideas. The more neutral they can keep America, the less ample will be the authority of Washington over them; and they profoundly fear, as Mr. Kennedy's speeches have made evident, the extension of its power. All this they feel the more acutely since the Hitler attack on the Soviet Union. For that attack is going to consolidate behind the President important elements in America whom they hoped to use to discredit the claims of labour in public esteem. Many of them had longed for exactly that attack on the Soviet Union which Hitler is making; and the difficulty, when Russia is in partnership with Great Britain, of supporting that attack, as a means of destroying working-class claims, is gall and wormwood to them. They would have been well content had the war been switched to a joint attack on Russia of the capitalist powers; that would have given an opportunity to destroy the growing faith of the workers—expressed in the United States by Mr. Roosevelt's re-election—in their right to use political democracy for economic welfare. As it is, they are confronted by a situation in which they know that the foundations of their privilege are in jeopardy.

I do not say that they will lose; I do not even claim that there will be some transformation of the American scene for the better. In a profound sense, there are no mutations in history; even great revolutions—1649, 1776, 1789, 1917—are only great opportunities which it takes generations to consolidate. Secular changes do not move on straight lines; they pursue a zigzag course. There is gain and halt, defeat as well as victory. But the gain and the victory come only when men see that the opportunity is there, and organise to take advantage of it. The tragedy of an attitude like that of Mr. Hutchins, and those who think with him, is the failure to see the opportunity. And, at bottom, the cause of that failure is a defeatism born of a lack of confidence in the people. It ought to be significant to Mr. Hutchins and Mr. Thomas that, ever since the rise of Fascism, it is the common man who has been anxious to challenge its claims, and the privileged who have sought to come to terms with it. It was the common man who saw, to use Mr. Hutchins' terms, that "justice, the moral order and the supremacy of human rights" were threatened by Hitler and Mussolini. Mr. Ford did not think so; Colonel Lindbergh did not think so; neither did Thyssen nor Weygand nor Darlan. In Britain and America the organised Labour movements have stood solidly for resistance; it was their urgency in Britain which swept appeasement on one side. It was their demand which replaced Chamberlain by Churchill because it recognised in the latter the symbol of its own will to resist to the end.

Mr. Hutchins and his associates among the Liberal neutrals cannot be so arrogant as to think that they only are aware of the risks of totalitarian warfare. We of the British Labour Movement who have undergone long months of ceaseless bombardment are not less aware of them. We have accepted controls and regulations the dangers of which we re-examine every day in the lives of our friends and neighbours. But we know, also, that those who will not take risks for liberty will never preserve it. We know that in the years before 1939 its foundations were crumbling before our eyes because our rulers hesitated to take those risks. We know that the passion for neutrality cost state after state on the European continent its independent life; that, until our victory liberates them, the rulers of those states are exactly the men whose rise to power men of Mr. Hutchins' outlook wish to frustrate. History shows only one way to retain respect for rights, and that is to meet with force those who use force for its destruction. To think otherwise is to abdicate, because it separates the thought from the deed which gives living reality to the thought.

No one can promise the neutrals of the Left that the defeat of Hitler will inaugurate Utopia. But there is no man of liberal outlook in Europe but can promise them that without his defeat there is no place for Utopia on the map of the future. Mr. Hutchins and his associates have got to make up their minds that in this half-rational and complicated world there is no straight road to the ends we seek, that we have to march side by side with unlooked-for associates as we move on. The great lesson we have to learn is the need to put first things first, not to fail by a quest for perfection that is not in the materials we are given. People of my way of thought have not entered upon this conflict without the full knowledge that the defeat of Hitler is only a stage in our journey. But we know that there can be no journey at all unless we pass this stage, that our victory is the condition of the right to continue on our way. When we have won there will be new problems, all the risks and dangers Mr. Hutchins enumerates. But it is surely a legitimate conclusion that the new problems can be faced only by men who have had the courage and the resolution to solve the old. To pretend that they are not there because they are ugly and difficult is a pitiful escapism which refuses to confront reality through fear. Timid men have never had a sight even of the Promised Land.

There is a third type of American neutral among the students of the United States about whom I would venture some comment. He sees the ugliness of war, the cruelties it unleashes, the passions which compromise even the highest aims of those who wage it. The best solution, he insists, is a peace without victory. The world cannot afford another Versailles; there is the danger that it may have one. The duty, therefore, of Great Britain and the Soviet Union is to find terms upon which the war can be ended now without the prolongation of its agony and destruction. Some of the friends I value most in the United States take this view strongly; and I know at first-hand how noble are the emotions which have compelled them to it.

But it seems to me an impossible view for two reasons. It is impossible to make peace with Hitler so long, first, as the major part of Europe is under his control, and so long, second, as he retains the weapons of aggression in his hands. For the first means the extinction of the independence and freedom of almost all the nations of Europe; and the second means, on all evidence, that, at the moment of his own choosing, Hitler will renew the effort to bring about his new order.

The first point, surely, is clear. Hitler could not afford, granted the political system he has built, to abandon his conquests; were he to do so the immense sacrifices he has imposed on the German people would have been in vain. That abandonment would recreate for him insoluble economic and social problems. It would mean, in fact, his overthrow; and there is no prospect that he will accept a peace that risks his downfall. To restore to independence the nations he has overthrown would make entirely futile all the methods by which he has maintained his authority. "All the world," Dr. Ley said has, "is to sweat for the German people." But the world will not do so unless it be enslaved to Hitler, and, to be enslaved, it must be conquered. Great Britain could not, from the angle both of honour and of interest, accept that position. Hitler could not surrender it without ceasing to be Hitler.

And how could any nation, in the light of our massive experience, accept the word of Hitler in making peace? The history of Austria; the history of Spain; the history of Czecho-Slovakia and of Poland; the broken pledges of peaceful intention to Scandinavia, the Low Countries, and the Soviet Union; the years of constant asseveration that he had "no further territorial ambitions"; the grim record of broken treaties; the consistent glorification of war and the deliberate gearing of the German economy to its making; the refusal to halt even after the shameful surrender to him at Munich—is not all this evidence that, so long as he disposes of German power, no nation may safely trust to his word?

If it is argued that, once he made peace, his own people would deal with him, there are, again, two things to be said. First, it is obvious that so long as he controls the state-power of Germany, his people cannot deal with him; that, surely, is evident from its long acquiescence in his tyranny. And, second, there is no way in which he can be deprived of his control of the state-power of Germany save by military defeat. We are in the dilemma that he will not make an honourable peace, because that will deprive him of the prestige upon which his authority over the German people depends; and there is no method of destroying that prestige save by defeat in the field. Those who think otherwise must explain why and how Hitler would be willing to transform a militarised Germany under his absolute domination into a peaceful Germany in which the means by which he has imposed his authority would no longer be available to him. A peaceful Germany means a Germany without Hitler; and a Germany without Hitler can arise only on the ruins of the system he has built.

If it be said that those who seek to prosecute the war to a decisive victory over him are, in the light of the last war, taking a fearful risk, the answer is that there is no alternative but to take it. A world he no longer overshadows has at least the chance of being a free and rational world; one that he dominates has no chance either of security or reason. The peace he offers is not only one of complete subordination to his power; it is one, also, in which the savage cruelties of the Nazi technique will be imposed everywhere upon the conquered. That is evident, for instance, in the tragic haste with which Vichy France has hastened to impose within its borders the barbarism of Anti-Semite legislation. It is evident in the relegation of the Poles to the status of an inferior race. It is evident, again, in the wanton destruction of all the cultural life of Czecho-Slovakia. Of course there are risks in the peace which will follow victory. But granted the price we should have to pay for a peace without victory, I do not see that any free man who understands the conditions of freedom can fail to accept the risk.

I am not, be it noted, asking the American student to take my word that Europe has learned the lesson of its past errors; that statesmen, even of a Conservative outlook, are far less likely, after this experience, to attempt a Carthaginian peace. I am prepared to put my case on the ground that the Europe of the Versailles Treaty, with all its follies and blunders, was an infinitely better and juster Europe than any possible Europe the character of which Hitler is in a position to determine. That is, I think, a legitimate inference not only from his treatment of the countries he has conquered, but even from his treatment of his own people. A world in which the Gestapo and the concentration camp are the methods which persuade to obedience cannot be other than brutal and ugly to any humane person. That was the widespread conviction of most American students when I was last in the United States. Since then, his methods have only deepened the loathing for him of decent-minded people. There is not an atom of evidence to show that, with peace, Nazism would change its nature. Rather do its unprovoked aggressions make it inescapable that it would merely prepare its legions for a new aggression.

So that, it will be said, you ask for American aid in a long struggle every day of which increases the chance of American participation. You ask American students to support a policy in which you must be aware there is the prospect of their death on the battlefield. They did not make the issues you seek to resolve. They need all their energies for their own grave problems in America. Yet you ask them to support the devotion of American treasure and perhaps American blood to a cause which is, after all, remote from direct impact upon their lives. There is, some students argue, an arrogance in this appeal which is unpardonable. The Europe which made its own misfortunes ought to overcome them by its own exertions.

I deny the remoteness of this impact. This is an interdependent world in which no nation can live to itself alone. There were statesmen in Britain who once believed that the civil war in Spain was "a faction-fight in which we were not interested"; they have now learned that it was the first act in an international civil war in which Guernica and Almeria were the prelude to Dunkirk and Crete. Stalin thought he could contract out of this war; he and Hitler swore a pact of peace that was to be eternal. We are contending with an enemy who aims at world dominion; and there is no people in graver danger than those to whom he proclaims his peaceful intentions. For there is no state involved in this struggle to which, at some stage since 1933, he has not given a solemn pledge of this kind.

But I deny the remoteness for other reasons. It cannot be a matter of indifference to America that half the civilised world stands on the brink of an enforced subordination. Were it to go down to the abyss, what safety would remain for the American way of life? We have tried the policy of refusing to be our brother's keeper; we know now how disastrous it is. American aid, in the light of our experience, is not merely generosity; it is also insurance. The Atlantic Ocean, the air over Britain, the Russian steppe, are very literally to-day the frontiers of the United States just as surely, could we but have known it in time, as the territorial integrity of China and the life of the Spanish Republic were our integrity and our life. This war cannot be compartmentalised; one's choice is not whether one takes part in it, but how. Men are either for or against the Nazi tyranny, and if they declare their indifference to it they are already its allies. For in the years of its preparation for this war it was above all through the blindness of the indifferent that it laid the foundation of its conquests. Whatever our distance from the actual theatre of conflict, we are all of us soldiers in the war it has imposed. It respects no boundaries if it sees an advantage in overpassing them. Its sole thought is how to gain the resources wherewith to dominate the world.

So that the American student who seeks to isolate himself from this struggle is seeking the impossible end of isolating himself from life. He cannot achieve it. He can hope for a world free from Hitler before there is need of direct American intervention; or, at the worst, he may hope that American intervention may not come too late to secure that free world. He has no other choice. He may feel that the fate is cruel which places him between these alternatives. It is the remorseless answer of history that this and no other is his fate. To have it otherwise he would have to blot out the major part of modern history all of which has gone to the making of this war. And, could he blot it out, he would have to forget certain American responsibilities which have gone to the preparation of this catastrophe —the desertion of Europe after Versailles, the hindrances to the free migration of peoples, the disastrous economic nationalism in which the United States has been a pioneer. It is hard for the American student that this should be his choice. I doubt if there be a single citizen in Britain who does not wish that it were otherwise. But it is playing with words to put the issue less starkly than the facts warrant. History tells us inescapably that if we wish the life of a free man we must pay for it, and that life itself may be the price. It has said so inexorably to a mass of European students in the concentration camps of Germany, on the battlefields of Europe, in terrorised Poland and Czecho-Slovakia, in occupied France. Quite literally they died that American students might be free; and they were no more responsible than these for the choice they had to make. It is in the name of what they died for that the call may come to American students. I think they will recognise it if it should be destined to come.

Five

Before the Nazi attack upon the Soviet Union there were many American students who, arguing in defiance of the facts that it made little or no difference to the working class of Britain whether they were ruled by Mr. Churchill or by Hitler, fell back upon the famous Leninist thesis of revolutionary defeatism. This, they said, was an imperialist war; the duty of a Socialist in such a war is to turn it into a civil war, to seize power on behalf of the people, and so make possible an enduring peace. The view taken by the British Labour Party, the view I wholly share, was that the major enemy was Hitler, and that until he was overthrown all other differences were unimportant by comparison. That was the view taken by the Communist Party of Great Britain until the outbreak of the war; and it has resumed acceptance of that view since June 22, 1941. I do not know whether American student ideas have undergone a similar change, where they were of this complexion. It is probable; though only a fortnight before the aggression on the Soviet Union by Hitler the *New Masses* was angrily denouncing me because I thought the Communist thesis an insult to the intelligence of anyone capable of seriously analysing this war.

I do not propose to indulge in recrimination. It is sufficient for me that, henceforward, until Hitler is defeated, he will now have no opponents more stout-hearted than those Communists who for twenty-one months pursued so tragically mistaken a strategy. But I think it important to explain why, since this war began, those who accept the thesis of revolutionary defeatism have wholly failed to understand its place in this struggle. For it is, alas, evident that the mechanical application of slogans invented for conditions in which they are wholly out of place has an irresistible attraction for the student mind.

The first question involved in the thesis of revolutionary defeatism is the conditions of successful revolution, for it is no use, as Marx warned us, attempting to play with revolution. Here some real precision is possible. For upon this point we have the evidence of Lenin, the outstanding architect of revolution in the modern world. A revolution, he argued, will succeed if (i) the armed forces of the state are no longer loyal; (ii) if the machinery of government has ceased to function effectively; (iii) if there is profound revolutionary consciousness among the masses, as shown by strikes and riots and demonstrations; and, finally, (iv) if there is an efficiently organised revolutionary party able to lead the masses to the conquest of power. These, it will be observed, were the conditions which prevailed in Russia in 1917. They followed upon a long epoch of corrupt and tyrannical government. They were accompanied by massive military defeat which turned both the army and the navy of Russia against the régime, and, even so, after Lenin and his party had seized power, they were only able to consolidate it because the war in which Germany was involved made it impossible for her to devote her full energies to the destruction of the nascent Bolshevik state.

It is not, I think, an exaggeration to argue that none

of Lenin's conditions is present in Britain to-day, and, further, that none of them is likely to develop save as the consequence of overwhelming defeat. In that situation, as the French position shows, it is the main probability that the character of the subsequent Government in Britain would be determined by Hitler and not by the revolutionaries. For it must be remembered that these have always protested the depth of their hostility to him, and the desirability of continuing the war unless he can be persuaded to accept a peace of no annexations and no indemnities.

Those who purveyed the Leninist formula postulated risks which it is impossible to exaggerate. They assumed that they could provoke a revolutionary situation in Britain without incurring the danger of a Hitler victory. To get that situation they would have had to try to undermine the loyalty of the armed forces, to have made impossible the smooth functioning of government, and to have provoked strikes on a scale able to jeopardise that continuity of industrial production essential to the waging of modern war. Is it not clear that, had they been able to do these things, they would have given Hitler the supreme chance of successfully invading a Britain divided against itself?

But this is not all. The proponents of revolutionary defeatism argued that the conquest of power by the workers in Britain would have been the prelude to European revolution; for Hitler and his satellites would have been prevented by preoccupation with their own internal problems from interference. I do not see what ground there is for this assumption. The Russian Revolution did not incite the workers of Imperial

Germany to revolt against their rulers until after the German armies had sustained colossal defeats; the overthrow of France has led to a Fascist state there, and not a workers' state. There is not an atom of reason for seriously supposing that the greatest of all Hitler's conquests would have led at once to the rising of his own people against him. Historically, it is the defeated dictator and not the triumphant dictator who is overthrown.

Nor was the argument substantial that a revolutionary Britain could, in its need, have counted upon the help of the Soviet Union. For, first of all, had the policy been pursued before June 22, 1941, it would have been pursued in a period in which the Soviet Union was bent on avoiding war; and, second, we have every ground for supposing that, from a strategic point of view, such help, had it been forthcoming, would not have been effective in time. The revolutionaries, in fact, would have had an impossible task. They would have been seeking at once to maintain their power over a deeply divided Britain, and to cope with the attack of the most formidable military state since Napoleon. Unless they had been able to seize power almost without a blow, they could not have assured the continuity of American supplies of munitions and food; and this would have meant a rapid development of a position in which they would have had to capitulate to Hitler's demands. He, certainly, would not have permitted their retention of power.

For the American student who thinks that the transformation of an "imperialist" war into a civil war involved any risks less than these is gravely underestimating the problems with which that transformation would have confronted Great Britain. He must realise that only by revolution could what its proponents termed a "People's Government" have come to power; any constitutional means of doing so was not seriously open to those who think in these terms. For, obviously, if the present House of Commons were to defeat the Churchill Government, it is not the forces of the Left by whom this House would replace it. If conditions compelled the secession of the Labour Party from the Government, a general election might well, indeed, become necessary; and it is, of course, possible that the forces of the Left would be successful at the polls. I think it unlikely, for both technical and psychological reasons; but it is at least possible. But a victory of the Left would mean a Labour Government committed by a great majority to prosecuting the war until Hitlerism is overthrown. Its emphasis, for that reason, would be towards the maximum possible preservation of national unity. The chief danger against which it would have to organise safeguards is that which led the forces symbolised by Pétain to prefer collaboration with Hitler to evoking the dynamic of democracy.

But there is, of course, no certainty that the Labour Party would emerge victorious from a general election. Under any circumstances, its hazards in wartime, especially in such a wartime as this, are very great. Not only is it bound to jeopardise the unity of the nation, itself a vital factor in victory; it also diverts the energies of the whole country, above all of its political leaders, from the effective prosecution of the war for something like two or three weeks. It would be conducted, owing to air-raids, and the consequences of evacuation, in circumstances for the most part unfavourable to the Labour Party. As a method of national decision, it could only be justified if the differences between Mr. Churchill and the Labour Party provided no legitimate basis for co-operation between them. That could only be if they were convinced (i) that Mr. Churchill was no longer anxious to win the war, or (ii) that the methods he proposed were incompatible with victory.

This is to say that there is no greater danger to Britain at the moment than that which Hitler represents. Where he conquers, there all for which the Labour Movement has historically stood is quite literally destroyed. To take any action, therefore, which seems most likely to ensure his victory must seem to a Socialist utterly unjustifiable. I do not deny that this involves the Labour Party in compromises on policy some of which—that over the government of India, for example—are hard indeed to bear. I do not deny, either, that coalition with one who, like Mr. Churchill, is a formidable opponent of Socialist principles, means incurring risks for the future. But those risks seem to me far less than the alternative involved in pursuing a policy of which a victory for Hitler is the necessary outcome.

For that is the choice which history has offered to the British Labour Party; in any realistic sense there is no other choice. To speak, as our Communists used to speak, as though we have only to break with Mr. Churchill and either, by forcing a general election, or by that mysterious authority which is usually left vague as the "massed power of the workers," a Government of the Left would swing into power, is to be blind both to the facts of the British situation and to the opportunity with which we should thereby provide our enemies. The Churchill Government has made its mistakes, some of them big mistakes; but there is no alternative in sight which could replace it and command so large a measure of public confidence. We cannot in this war afford to create political and administrative confusion and hope to maintain the unfettered strength of our forces in the field. The policy of revolutionary defeatism is a plain invitation to gamble with the independent existence of Britain. We should never be forgiven if we accepted it.

Nor, I must add, is this view weakened by the fact that the chief advocates of revolutionary defeatism concealed their real purpose beneath a mask of fair words. The points of the People's Convention Movement were all within the ambit of the Labour Party programme, and they emphasised objectives to which no Socialist could take objection. But, regretfully, I do not think the movement was intended to strengthen the effort of our people against Hitler. It was notable that the Convention did not even mention the need for his defeat. It did not do so for the sufficient reason that, when it was summoned, the defeat of Hitlerism was not the primary purpose of its real sponsors. Their purpose, at that time, was the very different one of breaking the hold of the Churchill Government on the allegiance of Britain in order to be able to turn the "imperialist" war into a civil war. That was why everything relating to the war itself was left so vague; Mr. Pritt could only say that the terms of its peace proposals would be "no annexations of any country by any country. No indemnities by any country to any country. The peoples to determine their own destiny and their own form of government"; though he did not explain how Hitler was to be brought to accept these proposals. Mr. Pritt, no doubt, as his books have sufficiently shown, is a very simple-minded person. But his associate in the movement, Mr. Palme Dutt, who replaced Mr. Pollitt as the outstanding leader of the Communist Party, is far from simple-minded; and he could not for one moment have believed that Hitler would accept such terms.

For, very obviously, these terms mean the overthrow of Hitler; and he is not in the least likely to connive at the conditions of his own downfall. So that even if the "People's Government" came to office it would have to go on fighting Hitler until those terms became possible. Nowhere did the advocates of this policy explain how this could be done; they did not explain it because they could not explain it. To the argument that it risked the danger of a successful invasion of Britain Mr. Dutt could only reply—it is hard to believe that he was serious—that the fear of invasion was simply a bogey invented by Mr. Churchill to frighten the workers into submission. That is a reply on a par with the assertion of those Americans who supported these views that the British warning to Stalin in the week before Hitler's attack on the Soviet Union was obviously propaganda, since such an attack must inevitably be preceded by an agreement between Hitler and Britain. It is on a par with Mr. Pritt's naïve faith that the coming of a "People's Government" to power in Britain would bring it "the most powerful allies in Europe—the working class of every country." He could not have seriously thought that the workers of those countries which Hitler now dominates could move to his overthrow save as the shadows of his defeat begin to lengthen. Nor could his Communist friends have believed that there was some mysterious constitutional way in which the "People's Government" would come to power. For it was the essence of their case that the Churchill Government was a Government of vested interests, of the ruling class of Great Britain, and that such a Government never voluntarily surrenders its authority.

It is probable that, with the entrance of the Soviet Union into the fight against Hitlerism, we shall hear no more of the People's Convention Movement. Those who sponsored it are now anxious that the British Government shall have maximum aid for the common victory. But it is important to note that, at its height, it was a deliberate attempt to exploit the miseries which war brings in its train for revolutionary purposes, even though that exploitation might have risked the victory of Hitler. No doubt this was not true of many who lent it their support; it was certainly true of those who decisively determined its objectives. They were prepared to risk a Hitler victory because they were convinced that, in the end, a revolutionary triumph was assured; and they were so blindly led by their mechanical faith in slogans that they did not bother about the absence of the only conditions which could give them that triumph. They conveniently forgot all that they had said of Hitlerism before the German-Soviet treaty. They produced no vestige of proof that it had changed its nature in the interval. They drew no rational inferences from its ability, wherever it has conquered, to destroy all prospect of working-class resistance. They refused to recognise that the external danger Hitlerism represents to working-class freedom is far greater than any internal danger by which that freedom is threatened to-day.

All this, of course, has changed since Hitler tore up the German-Soviet agreement of August, 1939. But it is an experience which ought to warn the American student of the Left that it is bad Marxism to apply the strategy invented by Lenin for the Russian circumstances of 1917 to the utterly different circumstances of Britain in 1941. Even if he regards Mr. Churchill as the incarnation of British imperialism, and that, in its turn, as an evil to be destroyed, his business, in this conflict, is to consider whether the defeat of Hitler or the defeat of Britain is the major historical necessity for the working class. He was told by the Communist Parties that Hitlerism was the major evil until August, 1939. Then followed the decision of Hitler to strike first at the West; and he was told that the war was an "imperialist" war to which, despite all the changes since 1917, he must apply Lenin's formulæ. When the depth of British resistance and the growing volume of American aid compelled Hitler to strike at the Soviet Union that he might replenish his diminishing resources, the "imperialist" war became, overnight, a Holy War against the Fascist beast; at this stage, it was no longer enough, in Mr. Pollitt's happy sentence, "to mouth revolutionary phrases." We were back to the period before the conclusion of the German-Soviet agreement; and the formulæ of Lenin were discarded as obsolete. They had never, in truth, been applicable to the scene.

For the fact is that imperialism in its Fascist phase—and this is the phase that Hitler symbolises—is able, while it is undefeated, to break the very foundations of working-class resistance. That is the essence of its technique. It overthrows capitalist democracy because it dare not face the consequences to capitalism of democratic institutions. To compensate for their overthrow it embarks upon a policy of expansion by conquest. It is therefore folly inconceivable to confront imperialism in its Fascist phase with the policy of revolutionary defeatism unless that imperialism is tottering to its fall. To do so is political adventurism of an utterly irresponsible kind. The workers cannot hope for the conquest of power unless they have a reasonable chance of victory and the time and conditions which permit its consolidation. While Hitler remains the armed master of most of Europe no such hope is possible for them; and they can only expect to have that hope when the purposes he stands for have been destroyed. That, therefore, is the primary task of anyone who sees how evil those purposes are.

Six

"ALL this," the American student may say, "has relevance only for those of a Left cast of mind. You admit the danger of democratic institutions to a capitalist way of life. Why should an America that is fundamentally capitalist in complexion seek to aid in preserving institutions which threaten its own ethos?"

It is a fair question, which deserves a carefully reasoned answer. To make it, I must assume that the student agrees that a social system is justified by its power to provide a satisfactory life for its citizens. I must assume, further, that he accepts as necessary what President Roosevelt has called the four essential human freedoms—freedom of speech and expression, religious freedom, freedom from want and freedom from fear. If he does not agree with those assumptions I cannot argue with him. By denying their validity, I add, their universal validity, he is already committed to an order based upon some kind of special privilege, to an outlook which has kinship with the ends that Hitler pursues. He may seek those ends for Americans rather than Germans; that is a matter of indifference. Once he rejects the policy implied in my assumptions there is no rational way of settling our differences.

But if he does accept these assumptions, I think he can see why their defence against Hitler's attack implies not only, say, a common ground between President Roosevelt and Philip Murray, Mr. Churchill and Ernest Bevin, but between Great Britain, the Soviet Union, and the United States. We seek within our national communities to achieve those freedoms. We cannot achieve them if we lie under the constant shadow of Hitler's threat to conquer us and thus to deprive us of the power to achieve them in our lives. We see that where he conquers, this deprivation occurs. We compare the Czecho-Slovakia of Masaryk and Benes with the Czecho-Slovakia of Neurath, the France of the Third Republic with Vichy France. The threat to-day is to ourselves and the Soviet Union directly; to you, I admit, it is an indirect threat. But if we go down, it becomes the main factor in your lives; and the fear and insecurity by which we are haunted will hang over you also like a constant nightmare.

"You defeat Hitler," the American student replies, "but then there re-emerge all the differences which previously divided you from Mr. Churchill. They may, by the conditions implicit in this conflict, even emerge in more acute form. You stand together to-day. But to-morrow you may find yourself on opposite sides of the barricades."

That is a possibility. The defeat of Hitler does not mean the certainty of a peaceful solution of all social problems. It means only, in the first instance, that the major threat to such a solution has been removed. I believe myself that the choice before our generation is, in fact, a choice between a revolution by consent and a revolution by violence; and I do not for one moment deny that to secure the first is as difficult and as rare an achievement as any in history. The war itself is inexplicable unless we admit that we have reached one of those stages in history where the relations of production are in patent contradiction with the forces of production. To adjust them peacefully by the methods of democracy is certainly hard, and, perhaps, impossible. It is asking men on the plane of property relations voluntarily to abdicate from the possession of privilege. No inconsiderable part of history is the record of their refusal so to abdicate. The attitude of Mr. Ford to the Wagner Act, labour relations in a city like Los Angeles, Union "racketeering" in the building trades of New York, all of these show how limited is the power of reason over men's minds. The class-war was not an invention of Marx; the perception of its grim reality is as old as Aristotle. Democratic institutions may mitigate its intensity; the history of the New Deal is the proof that they do not abrogate it. Nor can it be abrogated in any society, whatever its political forms, so long as men have interests so widely unequal in the results of the social process. Particularly, it cannot be abrogated when, as in our own period, the contradiction between the forces and the relations of production are so intense as now. Had it been less intense, Hitler would never have come to power in Germany. Had it been less intense, an expanding economy would have found a way out of war.

So that if the American student is seeking to fix, as it were, the present phase of economic relations in a perpetual frame of the capitalist democracy he knows, and it may be approves, the answer is that aid to Britain and the Soviet Union will have no such result. No frames of social organisation are perpetual. They quicken and die as they are able fully to exploit the forces of production at their disposal. I should be dishonest if I did not affirm my own conviction that the present frame of social organisation is incapable any longer of that full exploitation. That is the reason of the profound malaise we felt all over the world in the inter-war period. That was why values decayed, faiths were abandoned, continents were swept by the whirlwind of crisis and unemployment. The aggressor nations in this war have sought to end the malaise for their own peoples by enslaving the rest to their interest. They hope, by so doing, to preserve a little longer the privileges of their ruling class. But I do not pretend that the defeat of their effort to enslave the rest of us will end the crisis of our generation. It will remove the most hideous aspect of it, the most cruel and the most repressive. It will still leave us with the problem, all over the world, of adjusting the relations of production to the forces of production. We shall still have to decide by what means, constitutional or revolutionary, in our national communities, the adjustment has to be made.

I myself believe that there is a chance, small, it may be, but real, that the adjustment may be made in the remaining democratic states by consent granted that they are victorious in this war. I believe this for several reasons. First, I think that, in general, the revolutionary character of this war has made men of all conditions readier to accept great social experiments than was the case before its outset. Secondly, I believe that the masses are more determined than at any time to use their political power to enforce the economic changes which have become essential. Thirdly, I am convinced that those who have shared in common the immense dangers we shall have come through by the time victory is won will have learned something of the lesson of the inter-war years that national survival depends upon the ability to maintain the great ends of life in common, and that we think too differently if we live too differently.

Of all this, I say, there is a chance; I do not claim that there is more than a chance. The power of men to blind themselves to the causes of things is very great. Their willingness to perpetuate great wrong that they may maintain their power is very great also. The danger that interest may close the mind to rational argument will be obvious to anyone who reflects upon the habits of men. There is the power, in our hands, under a democratic system, as President Roosevelt has said, "to adjust ourselves to changing conditions, without the concentration camp or the quicklime in the ditch." There is the power. But there must be, also, the will to use that power, and the conditions, the President's four freedoms, without which it has but little chance of effectiveness. But no one can promise the American student the certainty either of that will or of those conditions. All one can say is that we have, if we choose to use them, the necessary knowledge and insight to plan a civilisation of plenty.

At this stage, the American student may ask for a further assurance. He is urged to support all aid to Britain and the Soviet Union, short of war; he is urged to support it in the knowledge that the giving of it may mean involvement in the war itself. How can he be sure that a victory over Hitler will be used for purposes of which he can approve? I answer at once by admitting that, in an absolute sense, there can be no such assurance. But if his demand means that we shall do all that human effort can do to safeguard the world against the use of war as an instrument of national policy, we are, I think, entitled to his confidence. For there are certain things he ought to recognise. In the years before 1939, if in very different ways, the policy of Great Britain and the Soviet Union was to avoid war at all costs. The means taken, in both cases, were mistaken; the motive in both is undeniable. It is the case, further, that, in the period from 1931 to 1939, not merely the British Labour Party, but, also, Mr. Churchill and some of his outstanding Conservative supporters, were the vigorous proponents of that policy of collective security which would alone have prevented the outbreak of war. That this is the case is not the affirmation of partisan propaganda; the speeches and declarations which prove it are on record. That something, too, has been learned from the bitter experience of this conflict is clear from the Anglo-Russian treaty and the vital improvement in Russo-Polish relations. So, also, from their common suffering Poland and Czecho-Slovakia are building a new and healthier basis for their post-war relationships. It is obvious, further, that with victory China, in some aspects the most hardly treated of all peoples, will enter upon a new phase of creative independence; for the doom of Japanese aggression is writ large in the defeat of Hitler.

The men, on the British side, who are responsible for the conduct of the war are those who, before its outbreak, were recognised by even their sternest critics of the Left as the men whose policy was most likely to prevent its coming. That is at least a basis of hope for the temper in which they will approach the problems of the peace. If it be said, as I admit it is freely said, that the principles of Mr. Churchill's political philosophy do not imply an adequate understanding of those problems, that those whom he represents will still seek to maintain the British imperial tradition, there are, I think, two answers. First, the British imperial tradition is not an unchanging thing, and there is good in it as well as evil. It is not unchanging; the evolution of Dominion status, the recent policy of West Indian development, the establishment, in wartime, of the ten million pound fund for colonial improvement, are the proof of that. It is not devoid of good as well as of evil; it could not have rallied to its side the loyalty it has evoked throughout the empire had it been otherwise. And, second, it must be remembered that the British Labour Party is committed to ending what there is of evil in the tradition and that its influence is bound to be a factor of pivotal importance in the making of the peace.

I say that to American students recognising to the full all that it implies. They are dissatisfied with the record of British labour in India and the colonies. They desire a more rapid and more active recognition that their peoples are entitled to determine their own destiny. I accept that criticism; I think its substance valid. My answer is the vital answer that the movement of India and the colonies to self-government is one that, given our victory, it is not in the power either of Mr. Churchill or of the Labour Party in a fundamental way to arrest. For forces are in operation there which transcend the capacity of either to do more than delay the achievement of a way of life acceptable to them. I admit, and I do not condone, the blind prejudice of Mr. Churchill against Indian self-government. I admit, and I do not condone, the grave unwisdom of the Labour Party in acquiescing in that blindness. But I am entitled, at this stage, to ask two questions of American students. Is it on the evidence likely that the defeat of Great Britain would hasten the achievement of self-government in India and the colonies? Is it not, on the contrary, certain that they would, in that event, become the victims of new imperialisms, in the West and in the East, more repressive and more grimly rapacious than ours has been in the forty years, say, of this century? And is not the transformation, too slow, I agree, yet on balance unimstakable, of the British imperialist system into an association of free commonwealths the outstanding characteristic of its evolution in those years? Is not a Socialist, therefore, entitled to argue from the evidence that the forces in historic play implicate, in William James' phrase, the progressive march of the subject peoples provided only that their development is not arrested by the creation, with a Hitler victory, of a new imperialist pattern, ruthless and expanding, which sets itself to deal with the claim to freedom as it has dealt with it in Europe, or as Japan has dealt with China? And, not least, American students will remember that Hitler's view of the coloured peoples is not likely to encourage, on their part, any effort towards emancipation. We may have scourged the subject peoples with whips; on the record, a victorious Hitler would scourge them with scorpions.

Seven

We are asked by American students to define our war aims; and there is complaint that we have not put forward the blue-prints of the new age after victory has been won. Yet it is, I think, true to say that the whole British Commonwealth of Nations accepts as axiomatic the approach to social and economic problems, which, as President Roosevelt has said, "are the root cause of the social revolution which is to-day a supreme factor in the world." It is, I think, axiomatic that his four essential freedoms are accepted as necessary by the Commonwealth also. No party in the British state dare, after victory, approach the electorate without a pledge to conquer mass unemployment, to prevent the re-emergence of distressed areas, to prohibit either the ground landlord or the speculative builder from profiteering in the rebuilding of Britain. We know that we have passed into that phase of social development where a planned society is inescapable. We know that economic security for the individual is to be the keynote of our planning. We are aware, thereby, that liberty must be set in the context of a growing equality. Over the methods by which we reorganise our foundations we shall no doubt quarrel, and even fiercely. It may be that we shall find that there is no way to common agreement upon them. But, overwhelmingly, it is our view that we must seek those compromises between differing political philosophies which enable men to live together in peace, if they can be found. Perhaps we shall discover that they cannot be found. But at least we insist that it is an obligation to our dead to exhaust the utmost possibilities of constitutional and democratic action before we travel the revolutionary road. And we believe that solutions made by democratic consent prove, in the end, to be more lasting than those imposed by the coercion of violence.

I emphasise this because it bears very deeply upon the mood in which we approach the future. Ours is a class-society; and the state which is its supreme instrument of coercion uses all its power, even when its political form is democratic, to protect the interests of the ruling class in the society. It is tempting to insist on the impossibility of compromise with it, and thence to infer that one's essential task is the preparation of revolutionary action. I yet believe that, in our circumstances, this is a mistaken strategy. It is necessary, no doubt, in a society where the right of opposition is denied; it is still more necessary where, as in Germany or Italy to-day, those who deny the right of opposition are a set of gangsters without pity and without conscience. But where the opposition has the chance of securing by constitutional means the authority of the state, and using it to re-define class relations in the society, I believe that it is a moral obligation upon those who think, as I do, that class relations need to be re-defined, to use those means so long as they can do so. No doubt, as a method of social change, this is less dramatic than the revolutionary way; it is at least as enduring. And it has, as a method, the supreme merit of avoiding the immense pain and bitterness the revolutionary way is bound to inflict. It does not for one moment deny that a Government with democratic constitutional authority behind it has the right, if challenged, to govern with determination. But it refuses to agree that those who seek to change the economic foundations of society should, in a political democracy, assume the inevitability of violence and prepare for its use. They must rely, for so long as is possible, upon the power of reason to prevail over interest.

That reliance does not mean either the abandonment of the right to govern, if constitutional authority can be secured, nor does it mean that, before it is won, the parties of the Left should allow their opponents so to weight the scales against them that they cannot use their power if they win it. We of the British Labour Party ought never to permit ourselves to be jockeyed out of power as we were in 1931; nor is it a violation of the democratic idea sternly to repress parties which seek to hack their way to power in the manner of Hitler and of Mussolini. British Socialism remains faithful to the democratic method precisely to the degree that its opponents respect it. I am aware enough that they may not do so, and that, not on the plane of forms merely, it is necessary to be watchful of their methods. But I say with emphasis that those who embark deliberately on the path to dictatorship embark deliberately on the path to moral deterioration. Ends can never be so separated from means as not to be transformed by them. Whatever the intentions with which the dictator starts, he is bound to be corrupted by the use of absolute power. The insistence of Jefferson that "every Government degenerates when trusted to the rulers of the people alone" has never been more fully proved than in our own epoch. That trust, therefore, must always be an ultimate expedient, and a temporary one, if it is not to be quite certainly abused. It may become necessary; but there should be no resort to it save in a period of desperate danger.

This does not mean, and the American student should understand that it does not mean, that the British Labour Party is concerned to maintain the character of "traditional" Britain, with its narrow class divisions and massive inequalities, as that Britain existed on September 3, 1939. It is concerned, if it can, to implement the Socialist principles for which it stands by the procedures of democratic consent; but, granted that it receives the authority of the electorate for its programme, it cannot allow the dissent of a minority, however vociferous and powerful, to stand in the way of its achievement. Those, therefore, who expect an effort towards no more than incidental changes in Britain as a consequence of this war must understand that we read no such implied condition into American aid. We fight for the right to shape our own destiny in the manner that the majority of our citizens approve; and we do not accept the right either of a minority here or in the United States to exclude the character of the property relation from the ambit of democratic control. Whatever aid, therefore, is afforded us by Americans must be given on the express understanding that this is the case. We pledge our faith to the democratic cause. We believe that its procedures are more creative in their power to elevate men than any alternative. But we are not committed to the fetish that a rich or privileged group in our society is for any reason entitled to turn us from purposes we are authorised to attempt by the threat to fight rather than accept them. That would indeed be a pitiful abandonment of the central purpose for which this war is waged.

Nor, as the British people wages it, is it thinking of itself alone. We agree that no nation can now live a self-sufficient life, that a world divided into a multitude of competing sovereignties is anarchy and not cosmos. With victory, indeed, we should impose an armistice which offered the maximum guarantees against the power of Hitlerism, or any variant of it, to renew its aggressions. But the peace treaty we should seek to assist in making would be built upon the recognition that enduring peace depends upon making universal as rapidly as possible the enjoyment of President Roosevelt's four freedoms. We have already argued that, in the making of this peace, the United States and the Soviet Union must be full partners; and to the latter power we have made it known that in no circumstances shall we be a party to any alliance or combination directed against its interests. Our victory, in a word, gives to the Soviet Union, as it gives to the United States, the opportunity fully to share in making the conditions of future international security. On the record, can the American student believe that such an opportunity would be forthcoming if Hitler won?

I do not, indeed, conceal my own view that the formulæ of international security are difficult of access; the struggle between reason and interest is not decided in a year or a decade. To disarm; to re-build and re-open the channels of international trade; to find through the miasma of passions this war has loosed adequate safeguards for minority rights; to determine principles for the free movement of peoples; to secure, in the light of existing possession, equal access to raw materials; to overcome what Sir Arthur Salter has well termed "the immense centrifugal force of national separatism"—these are, on any showing, immense tasks. They make it evident enough that the main conceptions in the minds of those who made the peace of 1919 were already obsolete when they sought to impose them. The cultural rights of a nation do not coincide with either its political or economic rights; we must recognise that nationhood is not a claim to state sovereignty, with all its implications. We must recognise, further, that, whatever be the sphere in which a nation is permitted the luxury of self-determination, there is beyond it a deeper responsibility to subordinate the making of military, political and economic decisions to the common needs of that *civitas maxima* in which each nation is but a province. Our loyalty to the national state cannot be all-embracing. To be a good British citizen, a good American citizen, each of us must learn that he owes an allegiance which is not exhausted by obedience to the commands of the British or the American state. It means learning that international obligation is the correlative of national right, that national self-interest is no more a final criterion of national policy than individual self-interest is a final criterion of human behaviour. Just as, in the domestic sphere, the doctrine of the "invisible hand" has led us grimly astray, so has the thesis that the nation is the natural bearer of sovereignty been the source of disaster and confusion.

The American student's mind is concrete and practical; he tends to want a formula within which his thinking may be conveniently contained. There are, at the moment, fashionable formulæ of this kind: Anglo-American Unity, Federal Union, and so on. If what I read from America is any index to what is deeply felt there, the American student feels a certain suspicion that there is no authoritative British endorsement of any of them. He tends to feel that, when the struggle is over and victory has been won, without explicit commitment to the blue-prints of a new world, our Government will cynically shrug its shoulders and go on as before. He looks at the world about him and is tempted to conclude that, as power has made right in the past, so it will make it in the future. Talk of a brave new world, on either side, seems to him no more than propaganda to enlist his support, talk that will be conveniently forgotten as soon as the issue of power has been settled. To what else, he asks, is Mr. Churchill committed but the single aim of victory? What but the power of which, with victory, he is able to dispose will decide the use to which it is put? He remembers the high discourse of President Wilson in the last war, and its bitter nullification in the inter-war years. The wise student's path, he thinks, is one of scepticism.

There is a sense in which he ought to be sceptical. There are too many unknowns in all the existing international equations to make any detailed commitments at the present time of any real value. We do not know what either the physical or psychological condition of

Europe—or Asia and the other continents, including America—will be at the end of this war. We do not know what new belligerents will be involved or what new revolutions may supervene. Detailed commitments are more than likely to be out of date before the ink of their signatures is dry. A blue-print made, for example, before the Soviet Union became the partner of Great Britain would have become obsolete after it. And, whatever the shape of the principles that are envisaged, they must, I think, have the character to which, in all inherent probability, validity is likely to attach not on the morrow of the armistice merely, but a generation after its signature. We cannot afford again to construct a detailed pattern which, like the League of Nations, withers away because its inherent principle is in contradiction with the shape of the facts about it. The more specific the commitments at this stage, the less likely are they to stand the strain of events a decade from now.

But that does not mean, I think, that we cannot put before an American certain principles of which he can approve. We can say, for example, that it is essential to maintain after the war all the working organs of co-operation between the states now fighting Hitler that have worked successfully during the struggle itself. Some of them are military, some political, some economic. All of them provide a more natural basis for transition to a new international order than an attempt to construct it on some brand-new juristic basis involving massive debates about the nature, for instance, of sovereignty or the permitted margins of neutral behaviour. Codification, I suggest, most usefully follows custom rather than inaugurates it. Federal Union is far more likely to succeed after a series of experiments in the pooled control of particular functions for a number of years than if it is stamped suddenly upon a Europe still reeling from the catastrophe of this war. We have some real knowledge of inter-allied staff co-operation; I think there is more promise in its gradual development than in proposals for the creation of an international army. We have some real knowledge, too, of how to co-ordinate currencies; I think it will be more helpful to deepen that co-ordination than to seek a world currency at a single stroke. We do not want, in the light of past experience, to build a structure of international institutions the power behind which does not seem natural and necessary to our children.

We must begin, and this is my second principle, to think in terms of the partial co-ordination of particular functions, rather than the total co-ordination of particular areas. It is less heroic, no doubt. It has none of the dramatic sweep of such a plan as that of Mr. Clarence Streit. But it is much more likely, I suspect, to gather behind it the will to enduring success. It is not insignificant in this connection that all formal attempts to give a juristic basis to the British Commonwealth of Nations have broken down; yet the reality of its empirical unity has been given magnificent demonstration twice within twenty-five years. It has survived strains and stresses which broke the League because its power to co-ordinate had grown out of a long and common experience proved valuable to those who shared in it. I know the attraction of a constitution for the world state, or European federation, or what not.

But, as a practical matter, I see no escape from the conclusion that constitutions of this character will only work when the parties to them have approximately equal interests in the results of their operation. Interdependence, at this stage of the world's history, is new, interstitial, incomplete. Its forms, therefore, must adapt themselves to those qualities. It is not for us, at the very dawn of its implication, to fit it out with a stiff juristic dress which it may shortly outgrow.

I do not believe this conclusion is invalidated, as the American student will be tempted to insist, by the history of the United States. There, no doubt, a single pattern was imposed successfully at a single stroke. But I observe two things. It is, in the first place, an experiment made in unique conditions far different in both time and tradition from those that we confront; and it required, in the second place, a civil war to deny the right of secession. One of the results of that civil war was to establish, as it were, an imperial dominion of the Northern states over the Southern from which, in their economic development and their cultural, the latter are only now beginning to recover. So rapid, moreover, has been technological change in the last thirty years that the rigidity of the American system has been a serious handicap to social justice in the United States; a distribution of powers made for agricultural communities one hundred and fifty years ago is now a barricade behind which the most reactionary influences of contemporary America defend themselves. American experience, even in its uniquely favourable circumstances, seems to me an argument for regarding federalism as an end-result and not as a beginning.

For whatever we can afford, we cannot afford a civil war to prohibit secession from our new international order. In a sense, that is the war we are fighting to-day; and it is a warning against, rather than an encouragement to, wholesale experimentation at the end of this war. Our modesty may prove, in this regard, our salvation.

The American student's scepticism, moreover, ought to be tempered by another consideration. There can hardly be a more fantastic view than that which looks for enduring peace in the chaos which would follow a British defeat. There can hardly be a serious doubt that the consequent dissolution of the British Empire would, on the contrary, lead to an epoch of wars and revolutions. There is no ground, either, for believing that such an epoch would herald the assured hour of proletarian triumph. If Lenin could be mistaken in his hopes of 1918, those of the epigoni are not likely to prove more fruitful. Is not the evidence, on every hand, rather convincing that the defeat of Britain would, in fact, usher in a new dark age? The struggle over the distribution of the spoils; the imposition by the conqueror of his known habits of discipline—do not these foreshadow, were they to occur, an economic and political slavery made more ugly every so often by the certainty of savage repression against the revolting slaves? That perspective is not altered when such slavery is called Hitler's "New Order." Over against it, as the alternative for which we ask support, is the opportunity to experiment in the creation of an international order based upon the security which free co-operation gives. If we take it, at its lowest, as a gamble, is it not a gamble more legitimately taken than that to which Americans are invited by Hitler and his allies, conscious and unconscious, in the United States?

It may be said that Britain had its chance in the inter-war period and abdicated from its obligation to lead. There is a real truth in that comment. Yet we must not forget that the Europe of the inter-war period, compared to what Hitler has made of it, was, for millions, a world of hope and promise, even of considerable achievement. Men could still believe in the Rights of Man. They could still give respect to the claims of reason. They could still seek to mitigate unnecessary pain; German girls were not yet sent to prison for an act of mercy to suffering Poles. There was no compulsion, enforced by Himmler and his Gestapo, to bow down before the grim idols Hitler has erected into gods. As we see it now, it was essentially an era of missed opportunities. But the opportunities were there. It is the fear and insecurity every action of Hitler has deepened tenfold which destroyed them. Can they return, the American student must ask himself, unless the fear and insecurity be removed? And can they be removed unless the threat that Hitler symbolises to the free exercise of the creative spirit be deprived of its empire over the minds and bodies of men?

Eight

I AM told that among a section of American students the democratic ideal is regarded as outmoded. It was, they think, the expression of a brief hour of human history that has gone now, never to return. It was possible to believe in the permanence of the democratic ideal in the brief hour of its triumph in 1918. Since then, events have increasingly proved that it was unsuited to the conditions of our age. The test of institutions is their power to survive; and the swiftness and the completeness of the democratic collapse show that democracy could not meet the test. The enthusiast for Pareto mutters some jargon about government by the élite. The exponents of Stalinism insist that the dictatorship of the proletariat—which, in practice, means the rule of the bureaucracy of the Communist Party—is, in some mysterious fashion, a more real form of democracy than we have known. In bodies like the Chambers of Commerce there are dark hints that what is needed is government by business men; and there has been a revival over wide areas of that view expressed succinctly by Alexander Hamilton when he said, "Your people, sir, is a great beast," and which Chief Justice Jay translated into a social philosophy when he argued that "those who own the country ought to govern it."

Now it would, I think, be pretty easy to show that Chief Justice Jay's thesis has always been broadly true: that those who own the instruments of production in any society do in fact overwhelmingly shape the habits of its governance.* But here I am concerned to enquire, briefly, why it is that faith in the democratic method has shrunk so swiftly and so decisively in the last generation. And the answer, I think, is the unmistakable one that the democracies failed to solve their economic problems, that they tolerated massive unemployment and widespread insecurity, that those who suffered from these were deprived of hope, and that they were deprived of it at a period when scientific and technological discovery had made our capacity to produce greater than in any previous age. The contrast between riches and poverty in a democracy will be tolerated by the masses if these are able to hope, have the sense, that is, that their material condition is being continually improved. But they will not tolerate it if, over a considerable period of time, they are deprived of hope, and the material improvements to which they believe themselves to be entitled are withheld from them. Unless these difficulties can be overcome within the framework of the existing order, the masses, in a democracy based on universal suffrage, will seek to use their political power to redress the economic balance in their favour. And if that effort be resisted, nothing is more certain than that they will cease to feel the old loyalty for forms from which they no longer obtain the results they desire. Or, it may well be, that their power to obtain those results so threatens the position of the ruling class that the latter prefer the overthrow of democracy to their loss of privilege.

Modern democracy, in the form in which we know it,

* *Cf.* my *State in Theory and Practice* (1933), Chapter 1.

was built upon that principle of individual freedom which the middle class required as the ideological strategy of its access to the possession of the state. Theoretically, its benefits were shared with the propertyless workers in alliance with whom the middle class won its victory. In actual practice, its benefits were limited to the owners of property save in so far as the fruits of economic expansion were shared as a concession to the workers from the owners of property. So long as there was expansion, so long concessions were made. So long as concessions were made there was hope, and the idea of democracy received a well-nigh universal approbation.

But the idea of individual freedom in the economic realm ceased to have validity when technological change transformed the fairly simple society of the late eighteenth and early nineteenth centuries into the highly intricate organism we know to-day. Its power to produce was incomparable; it had no such power to distribute, and the absence of that power meant a sense of frustration where, previously, there had been hope. That sense of frustration did not lead the owners of property to recognise that the principle of individual freedom in the economic realm now operated to deny to the masses the benefits democracy was supposed to secure. On the contrary, they clung to it the more fiercely lest its transformation should jeopardise the power they had obtained with such effort; and, as in Italy and Germany, and, in disaster, France, where they had to choose between the principle and the maintenance of a democracy which was certain to transform it, they preferred to abandon democracy. And, at the same time, the very fact that in Italy and Germany experience of democracy was relatively new meant that its experimental failure in the economic realm led a considerable part of the masses themselves to doubt whether it deserved the efforts which had been expended on its achievement.

The essential characteristic of capitalist democracy in its present phase has been put by Professor Carl Becker in words upon which I cannot improve. "The value of private property in the means of production," he writes,* "is thus not a private matter. It is both cause and effect in the functioning of a highly integrated and delicately adjusted industrial structure that touches the public interest at every point. That the few who control private property in the means of production should be wealthy men is no great matter. What matters is that their control of the means of production gives them an indeterminate and impersonal power over the lives and fortunes of millions of people unknown to them—power which they are sometimes unwilling, but far more often quite unable to use for the public good." To this should be added that the dependence of their authority on the ability to make profit, which, in its turn, depends, through the increased capacity to produce, on the ability to distribute, makes the breakdown of economic security and the expectation of increased material well-being ever more serious. For it not only threatens democracy, both from the Right and from the Left. Where, as in Fascist states, it is abandoned, it compels, by a dreadful logic, the search

* *Modern Democracy* (1941), pp. 55-6. The whole book is a brilliant exposition of its theme.

for markets by conquest that the new régime may somehow appease the masses upon whose support, in the long run, it has to depend. For though the Gestapo and the concentration camp reduce the German worker to a condition akin to industrial slavery, his masters must ceaselessly remember that even slaves rebel.

It is therefore clear that this war for freedom and democracy will, even if Hitler be defeated, only attain those ends if the democratic societies learn in time how to organise economic foundations which the masses are prepared to regard as tolerable. That they will only be able to do as they replace the principle of individual ownership in the economic realm by the principle of common ownership. For only as they do this can they expect to make their power to distribute proportionate to their power to produce. The present relations of production have exhausted their utility because they result in denying to millions the hope that is latent in our technological position. Without hope, there is no faith; and without faith there is bound to be the crisis in values which our generation has known. Such a crisis drives men to fear, and fear is the parent of irrationalism. Where that obtains any profound hold, the prospect of maintaining a democratic system is small indeed.

"There is nothing mysterious," President Roosevelt has said,* "about the foundations of a healthy and strong democracy. The basic things expected by our people of their political and economic systems are simple. They are: Equality of opportunity for youth

* Message to Congress of January 15, 1941.

and others. Jobs for those who can work. Security for those who need it. The ending of special privilege for the few. The preservation of civil liberties for all. The enjoyment of the fruits of scientific progress for a wider and constantly rising standard of living. . . . that is no vision of a distant millennium. It is a definite basis for a kind of world attainable in our time and generation. That kind of world is the very antithesis of the so-called new order of tyranny which the dictators seek to create with the crash of a bomb." But President Roosevelt would not argue that this "basic . . . simple things," so profoundly denied to the masses over most of the world, can come by some act of will operating *in vacuo*. They must be born of economic relationships in society which make the willing of their achievement a matter of common interest to the members of the society. There is not that common interest now, because the class structure of our society inhibits its emergence. And so long as that class structure remains unchanged, so long, to state it in another way, as we fail to set liberty in the context of equality, the objective conditions are wanting in which there can be agreement upon fundamentals. That agreement is the pre-condition of democratic survival. For when men hold the great ends of life in common, they will agree to differ peacefully upon matters of minor concern.

From this there follow two conclusions to which I direct the American student's attention. The first is, as President Roosevelt has said, that Hitlerism is incompatible with a "healthy and strong democracy." If it conquers, the prospect of achieving that democracy "in our time and generation" disappears. But the second conclusion is not less important. The defeat of Hitlerism is an opportunity for the achievement of such a democracy as President Roosevelt has described; it is far from the guarantee that it will be achieved. And here, as I think, the United States is entitled to enquire whether, in a profound way, the democracies are taking steps to build the relations out of which not only is Hitler's defeat made certain, but the foundations of democracy made permanently secure. It is not enough for the Churchill Government to bind up the wounds of its people, to make, here and there, concessions, often important concessions, by way of social reform. Those measures may bring military victory; but they will still leave unheeded and uncorrected the conditions out of which the phenomena of Mussolini and Hitler, not to speak of a host of lesser imitators, emerged.

If I could ask for one direction of emphasis from American student opinion, it would be to this aspect of our problems that I would turn it. For it is here, even in the ugly brutality of war, that there is opportunity as well as tragedy. Americans will, I think, agree that in these grave days, and in the face of tremendous odds, the people of Great Britain have shown unsurpassed courage and resolution. They have shown it in the service of the democratic faith. They are entitled, because of that devotion, to the assurance that the foundations of that faith be made secure. And there is no better time to make them secure than in these hours of danger when we learn so intensely that we are members one of another. Great leadership would take instant advantage of this mood of fellowship, this spirit that is ready for great experiment that the common danger has evoked. That is the insistent expectation from this country that I would wish to hear from American youth. The deeper the realisation that, as British democracy begins this response, the more certain it makes the process of world liberation, the greater its power to rebuild first hope, and, in its sequence, action, among the conquered peoples. Never has the influence of American opinion been so profound here as it is now; never, were it exercised in this direction, could it be more valuable in its results.

I do not think it is to misread the speeches of President Roosevelt to argue that, with the discretion proper to his high office, this understanding is implicit in what he has said. I do not think, either, that I misinterpret the influence that his remarkable Ambassador, Mr. Winant, is seeking to exercise when I say that it operates in this direction also. But neither the President nor the Ambassador can have the persuasive effect I should wish them to have unless it is strongly felt by our leaders, above all by Mr. Churchill, that behind their indications is the overwhelming conviction of liberal America that the President and his Ambassador are right. What I do not want to lose—as we lost it in 1914-18—is the mood adapted to great social changes deliberately set on foot. What I am certain of is that American opinion, wisely expressed, can help greatly to this end. What I fear is the confinement of American interest to enthusiasm for our victory without a constant reminder to us of the ends for which victory is to be used. The drama of the battle is so great that the distant spectator may forget the cause for which it is being waged.

If the American student asks whether I expect the

inauguration of such changes from a Government of which Mr. Churchill is the head, I confess to deep uncertainty. But I remind him of what, indeed, no one to-day needs to be reminded, that Mr. Churchill is a very great man. He saw the Nazi danger clearly and starkly on its first accession to power. He risked his political life to warn the whole world of those dangers. When the majority of our people welcomed the "peace" of Munich, he painted its tragic implications with sombre eloquence. When he took over the Premiership of his country the hour was dark indeed; not less certainly than our pilots in the Battle of Britain, he renovated its spirit and gave it new heart for the battle. He has courage in abundance, the power to inspire, the quality, high among the capacities a statesman needs, of imaginative audacity. As a people, we owe an immense debt to Mr. Churchill; "our finest hour" has been his too.

But Mr. Churchill is an aristocrat, Conservative in philosophy, living, as all but a few statesmen live, in the immediacies of the conflict. He belongs, too, to an ancient tradition in outlook, which, however honourable, is more narrow in its implications than the times require. The very width of his achievement in this time has placed him upon a unique eminence. His power to be argued with on equal terms is handicapped by that position. The strength of his mind has never lain in that economic realm which is every day more urgent; the measures he seeks for in that realm are, where they are meant to maintain morale, inspired by the aristocrat's compassion—the source of his Liberalism—rather than by the philosopher's insight. He has to be made to see the economic implications of this struggle, in the face of his own inclinations, of the pressure of the main force of his party, and his own constant preoccupation with others. of its aspects. Before such difficulties, is there any real chance that his attention can be won deeply enough or continuously enough for these concerns, to make him see them in time?

I do not share the view of those who say that, in the light of Mr. Churchill's past, of Tonypandy and the General Strike, it is impossible. I believe, first, that Mr. Churchill has the statesman's gift of adapting himself to new situations; and I believe that there is no change for which he is not prepared to be responsible if he can be made to see that it is directly relevant to victory in this war. After all, the man of the Russian interventions of 1919-20 is to-day the full-hearted and generous ally of the power he then sought to destroy; no greater adaptation of view than this is required from him. Nor do I believe that his party affiliations stand in the way of experiment he can see as necessary; for his status with the nation is such that he could achieve his end even in the face of pressure from his party. The problem is to capture for this need the ardour of his imagination and his capacity for intense interest.

What his Labour colleagues can do to this end, I believe they will do. What the movement behind them can attempt in pressure, it will not be backward in attempting. But neither of these influences brings with it either the freshness of emphasis or the vigour of innovation that are required. So much of what they say to Mr. Churchill sounds like the echo of forty years of debate in the House of Commons. He only half hears the quality of their argument. It is set always in the perspective supplied by the Central Office of the Conservative Party, warning him not to tamper with an allegiance that is still mistrustful of him, concerned to be sure that he is, at long last, a safe party man. There are the voices from the City, only half recovered from the "appeasement" period. There is the counsel of the prudent which tells him that these things can wait upon the fulfilment of more instant needs.

What is needed to give Mr. Churchill the requisite stimulus to new perspectives of action is a fresh and stiff breeze from across the Atlantic. It would not invigorate him only. It would stir up a debate amongst our citizens which has to be started sometime, and could not begin under better circumstances or under happier auspices. The British people do not need now any convincing of either the depth of American friendship or the mutuality of our interests. They know that counsel from such a source carries with it a special weight. And Mr. Churchill, with the instinct of genius, when he is interested, for the right moment, would know, none better, that the hour of decisive change had come. Done in the right way, and in the right temper, it would act upon him as that spur to the deed in which his most striking gestures are always expressed. What he requires is to be pricked into the urgency of thought upon matters which he has not yet learned to see in their due relevance to this war. What is required of him is that, learning that relevance, he makes the action proportionate to the need. Stirred to that effort, his great gifts of heart and head might combine to begin now not merely the renovation of that European past, which

Hitler has destroyed, but the liberation of that future he seeks to imprison. So only, as I think, can we fulfil the purposes of victory; for so only can we make certain of the free exercise of the creative spirit in man.

Nine

THE free exercise of the creative spirit; it is the idea those words embody that I would above all emphasise to those American students who may read this tract. I note, in the first place, how grimly few are the areas in the world to-day in which even the right to publish such a tract as this would be possible; I note, also, how much narrower would be the area of that possibility were Britain to be defeated. With all our weaknesses, with all our mistakes, despite all the stains upon our historic record, the battle for the free mind can still be fought in Britain; and more of its citizens than ever before are conscious that they are soldiers in that battle. Nowhere in the world, not even in the United States, has the power to comment freely upon public affairs remained so uninhibited or so determined.

That is not the least vital aspect of this conflict of which the American student must take account. After all, by the very fact that he is a student, his life is in some sort dedicated to the discovery of truth. He knows, or he ought to know, that its pursuit is an impossible task once authority is permitted to put the mind in chains. He knows, or he ought to know, that the attack on the free mind has been the centre of the relation between Fascism, in its various forms, on the one hand, and the universities on the other. I will not repeat the names of the scholars, honoured all over the world, whom the dictators have driven from the temples of learning. I will not, either, examine that distortion of the curriculum, above all in the social sciences, which has taken place in Germany and Italy that the new generation may accept only those doctrines convenient to their political masters. Ideas are no longer examined; theories are no longer discussed; they are imposed as an orthodoxy which has a new Inquisition at its disposal. The university has ceased to be a forum where teacher and student may speculate without fear of penalty. Place is the reward not of intellectual merit, but of an uncritical acceptance of dogmas beyond scrutiny. The heretic is the potential victim, too often, alas, the actual victim, of a tribunal more ruthless and more ignorant than any past religious creed has dared to set up.

I say with conviction that, whatever the stains upon the British record, we do not worship at that altar; defeat only could compel us to worship at it. Examine, as the American student is fully able to examine, our record in a war in which our very existence as an independent people is at stake, and it will be found, I venure to think, that no people in our situation has ever left free utterance so unfettered. Not least is this the case in British universities; Communist teaching and Pacifist teaching have alike their active and unpenalised votaries. The student is not asked to accept Mr. Churchill as a divinely appointed leader; he is not compelled to believe in, much less to preach, the historic primary of the British race. No one delates the dissenter from our general tradition to a power which exacts his spiritual "reformation." Neither Gestapo nor concentration camp awaits those who exercise their full right to free expression. I have sat in common rooms with teachers who have not hesitated to proclaim their faith that war is contrary to the mandate of Christ; I have attended meetings where Communist students have urged that truth has been vouchsafed to Moscow alone. Campaigns to demand a change in the Indian policy of the British Government; campaigns to insist that this or that order of the Cabinet must be withdrawn; denunciation of those who cannot see the need for an immediate offer of peace—these, and things like these, are all part of our everyday experience. There is a British censorship; but, under its ægis, the leaders of the Communist Party were permitted, while it seemed fit to them, to deny our purpose and to denigrate our cause. Those who oppose this war can hold their meetings, print their manifestos, run, if they choose, for Parliament. A war for freedom and democracy is being conducted in this country by the methods of freedom and democracy.

I ask the American student who doubts this to make some simple comparisons. Let him compare the proceedings in Parliament with those in the Reichstag or the Fascist Grand Council. Let him compare the British press with that of Germany and Italy. Let him, perhaps above all, compare the bearing and habits of our citizens with those of the dictator countries. Fear is not written across our lives; men are alert to express their grievances; none of our rulers is a sacrosanct personality. From Mr. Churchill to the least important member of the House of Commons the reality and importance of public opinion are recognised. It was public opinion which, at long last, compelled the Chamberlain Government to accept the Nazi challenge; it was public opinion which made Mr. Churchill Prime

Minister; it is public opinion alone which can break his hold upon the authority of the state. When he visits the bombed areas, his arrival is not preceded by a police clearance of suspicious characters. When he makes a speech, there is no organised applause for his words; nor does a controlled press demand from the public a dutiful and obsequious reverence. Mr. Churchill is the leader of our people, by consent, and not by coercion; and when and if that consent is withdrawn he will cease to be its leader.

Whatever the future may have in store for Great Britain we cannot know. All I am concerned here to argue is that the principles for which it fights to-day are those which, for so long as the memory of man can reach, have been the accepted principles of civilised living. So long as we hold, those principles stand firm; if we are victorious, they gain a new lustre in a deeper power over the minds of men. They are not, I must emphasise, principles which can live save as those who recognise their worth are prepared to defend them. They have been challenged often enough in the past, though never, perhaps, as seriously as now. A new barbarian is at the gates, more menacing, more strongly armed, more ruthless than any of his predecessors. Ever since he first drew the sword, thousands of Americans have asked whether Britain would submit tamely to his threats. There were grim days when they feared that its sons would prove unworthy of their heritage. There were times when human yearning for peace almost persuaded some to compromise with the enemy of civilisation. But the test was honourably met when it was unmistakably encountered. With neither civilian nor soldier, neither on the sea nor in the air, has there been any failure to meet all that it implies. We are not given as a nation, I think, to high words; our temptation is to shrink from the clear-cut definition of issues. But in this conflict we know, quite simply, that we must conquer or die.

I want the American student fully to grasp why the issue presents itself to a British Socialist in this way. I have no illusions about the price we shall pay for victory; I know that it will be heavy and hard. I do not profess that our triumph will build, quickly or easily, a new Jerusalem, here or elsewhere. On the contrary, I am keenly aware of the immense risks we run by setting our feet on the path that we have chosen. But I do not see, in the light of our past, that history leaves us any possible alternative. Victory will leave us with heavy burdens, a nation maimed and scarred. Once again there will be a missing generation, and the survivors will go on with a gap in their hearts that no achievement can ever fill. But victory will leave us free men and women, with the right, through our own ideas and acts, to shape our own destiny. Defeat will mean for all of us enslavement and dishonour, for some death or the torture of the concentration camp. For we know by grim experience the costs imposed by Fascism in all its forms. We have seen the corpses of its victims; we can still hear the cries of its slaves. So that though we know that we have been blind, though we admit that there are heavy sins to our account, we believe that we are fighting for our self-respect, and that life is not worth living unless we can maintain it. More than this, we believe that with our own self-respect history has indissolubly linked the ultimate freedom of mankind, yours in America not less than ours in Europe, so that when we ask for sympathy and encouragement from the students of America, it is for an end far greater than our own survival.

Great empires have perished before; and a new way of life has been built upon their ruins. Yet the new way of life that would be built upon our defeat offers no promise save of evil to posterity. It would be the rule of men who have hacked their way remorselessly to power, careless of suffering and incapable of pity. They have, where they could, poisoned the well-springs of truth; and where they could not poison, they have sought to destroy. They have no law save the satisfaction of their lust for power. They avow their contempt for justice as they boast of their denial of mercy. Along the path of their conquests lie broken peoples, deprived of dignity, with no hope save as their new masters are defeated. The intensity of their corruption is well known; their incapacity for fair dealing has been well established. They have no sense of shame. They know no way to hold men's loyalty save by self-interest and fear. The peace they impose makes a holocaust of freedom, since it is based on their deliberate will to imprison the spirit and conscience of man.

These are strong words; they are not less strong than the occasion requires. That is why I say to the American student that those who shrink from aiding the British cause align themselves with its enemies. There is no middle way in this war; the choice of one side or another is inescapable. We fight for the opportunity of mankind by its own will and its own energy to find the terms of its emancipation. Our enemies seek to impose upon it a servitude more deadly than any the modern world has dared even to imagine. We fight that ordinary men and women shall be recognised as ends in themselves; we hold, as Jefferson held, that "the mass of mankind has not been born with saddles on their backs, nor a favoured few, booted and spurred, ready to ride them legitimately, by the grace of God." Our enemies proclaim them the blind instruments of a state purpose they are not even permitted to examine. Our warning to the world is Lincoln's warning to the workers of America. "Let them beware," he wrote, "of surrendering a political power which they already possess, and which, if surrendered, will surely be used to close the door of advancement against such as they, and to fix new disabilities and burdens upon them, till all of liberty is lost." It is not accident that, where this surrender has taken place, Lincoln's prophecy has been literally fulfilled. That is why the vast majority of those who cherish freedom know that we are locked in a death-grip with the outlaws of civilisation. If we go down, it is the gangster who becomes the master of the world.

I have quoted Jefferson and Lincoln. I have quoted them because the ideas they fought for are part of a common heritage, one that we seek to defend to-day. History has set this generation the problem of safeguarding it, set it to you in America not less than to us in Britain. To be indifferent to the issue, to fail to realise its urgency, is to assist in endangering it. For the strength of the outlaws is nourished by every doubt which assails those who are called to the task of defence.

To the Fifth Column of their Quislings is added the even more dangerous sixth column of those who refuse to meet the issue in its stark simplicity. For we need the faith and energy of those who cherish the free mind, not to-morrow when the battle may be unleashed on your shores, but to-day when it rages over ours.

The American student, in a word, must recognise now that what is in jeopardy is alike his heritage and his future. These are assailed by men who care nothing for the civilised tradition, who do not shrink from destroying its possibilities. That is why we claim that this is a people's war from which the American student cannot turn aside. He has the right, as I have admitted, to remember our failures and our errors; he has a title, as I have affirmed, to exert all his influence to compel us to correct them. But he has the duty, also, to remember that his power to use that right and that title alike depend upon our ability, in concert with our allies, to win this war. A British victory does not mean the attainment of Utopia; but, at least, it prevents it from being wiped off the map. A British victory will leave grave problems to be solved, high issues to be met; at least, again, it does not leave mankind to confront them in chains. It still leaves standing a world in which men have the right to dream; to maintain that right as a living principle is a long step towards the fulfilment of the dream.